ingenious
# AWESOME DOT-TO-DOTS

## BEN ADDLER

SIRIUS

**SIRIUS**

This edition published in 2019 by Sirius Publishing, a division of
Arcturus Publishing Limited,
26/27 Bickels Yard, 151–153 Bermondsey Street,
London SE1 3HA

ISBN: 978-1-78950-117-9
CH007044NT
Supplier 29, Date 0219, Print run 8090

Printed in China

# INTRODUCTION

Here you will find more than 150 ingenious dot-to-dot images that will get your mind working and your hand drawing. These images have been carefully crafted to stimulate the brain, focus attention, and bring about a sense of calm and wonder.

Part of the fun is seeing how the lines slowly evolve into a familiar image as your pen, or pencil, progresses from one dot to the next. Whether it's a wonder of nature, a famous icon, a beautiful building, or something more mysterious, you'll be utterly drawn into a deep and soothing state of mind by this simple process of concentration.

Each image is made up of 300–400 numbered dots. Simply start by locating the first dot (this can often be a job in itself!) and let your line progress from one number to the next, in ascending order. Where there are images comprised of more than one continuous line, you will see that there are sometimes upper case letters, lower case letters and/or Roman numerals to delineate each separate continuous line. If the image still eludes you, you can always check the list of illustrations at the back of the book, but that will give away the surprise!

The journey begins with a sharp pencil or pen and a desire to discover. So sit down and take some time to let your brain enjoy these dot-to-dot journeys.

4

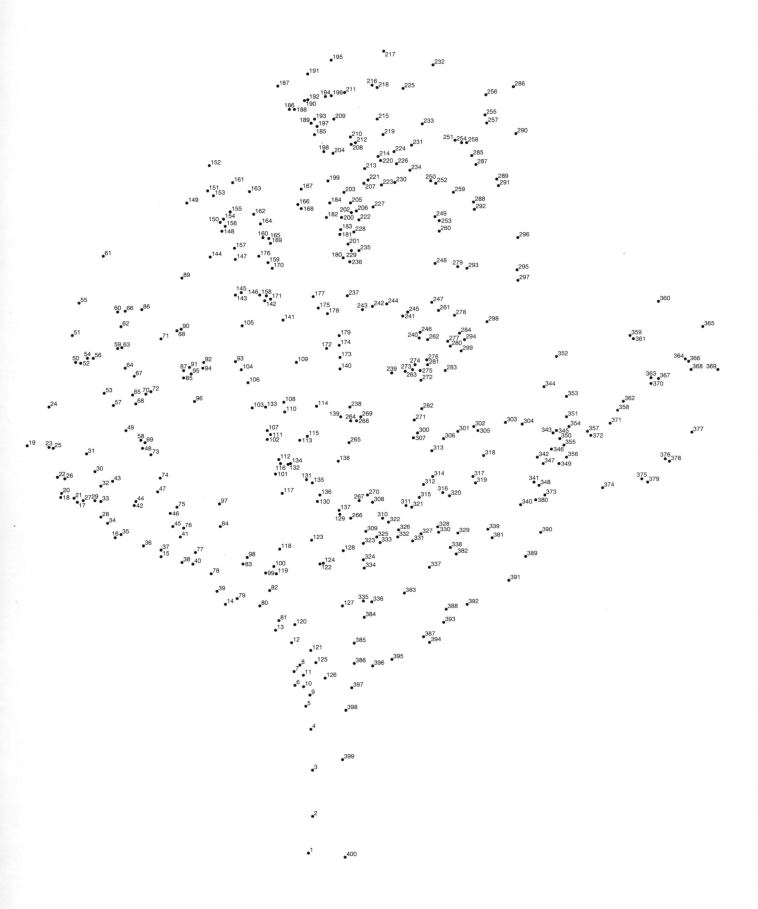

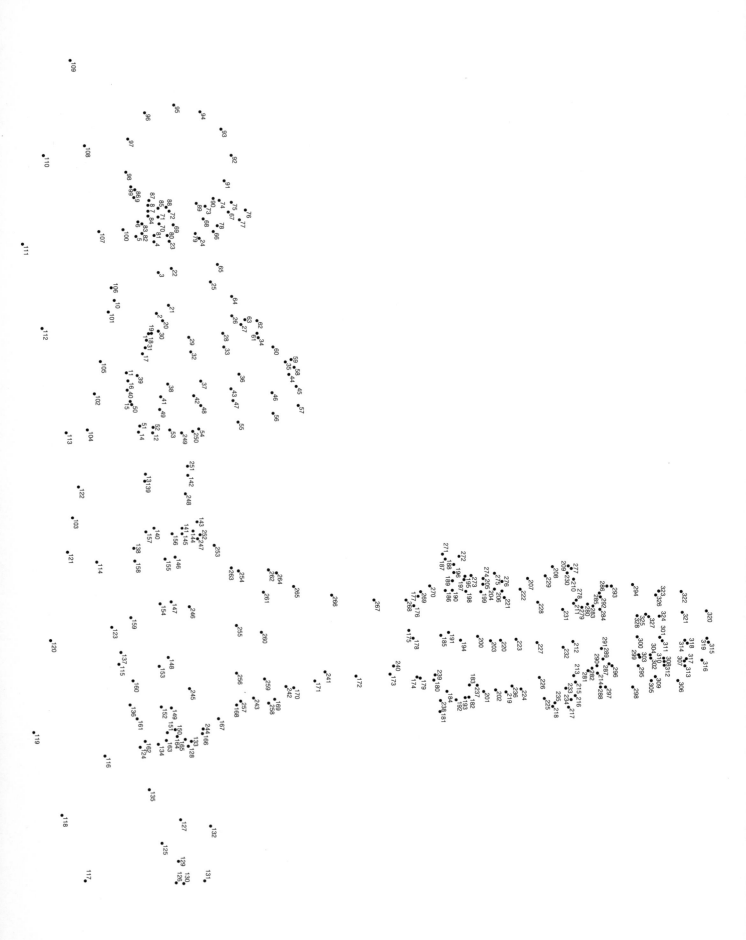

14

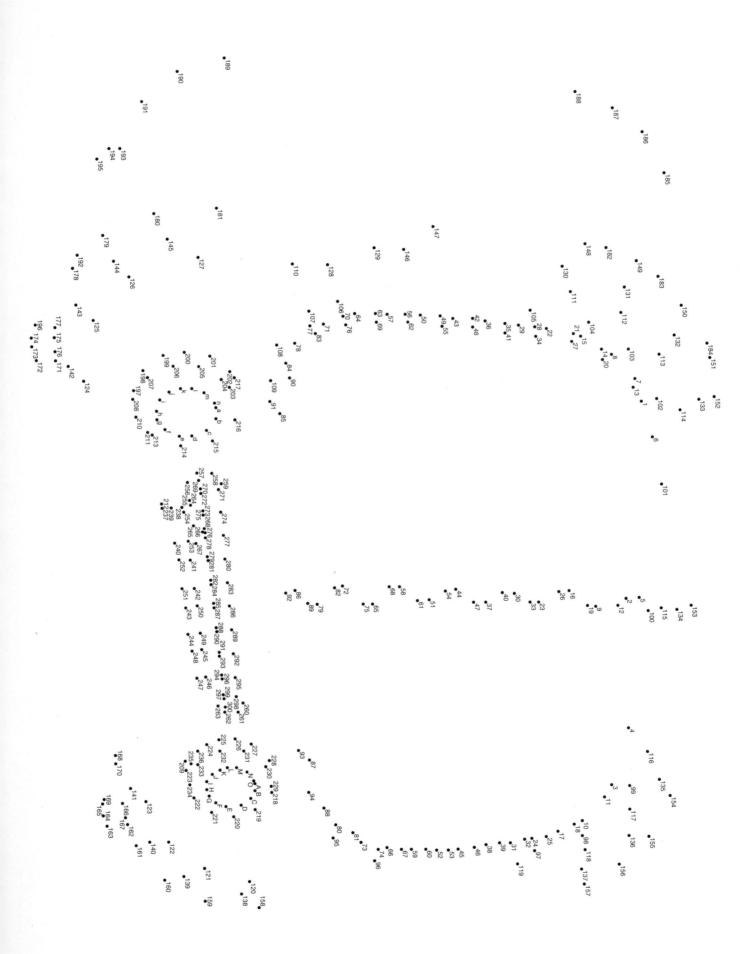

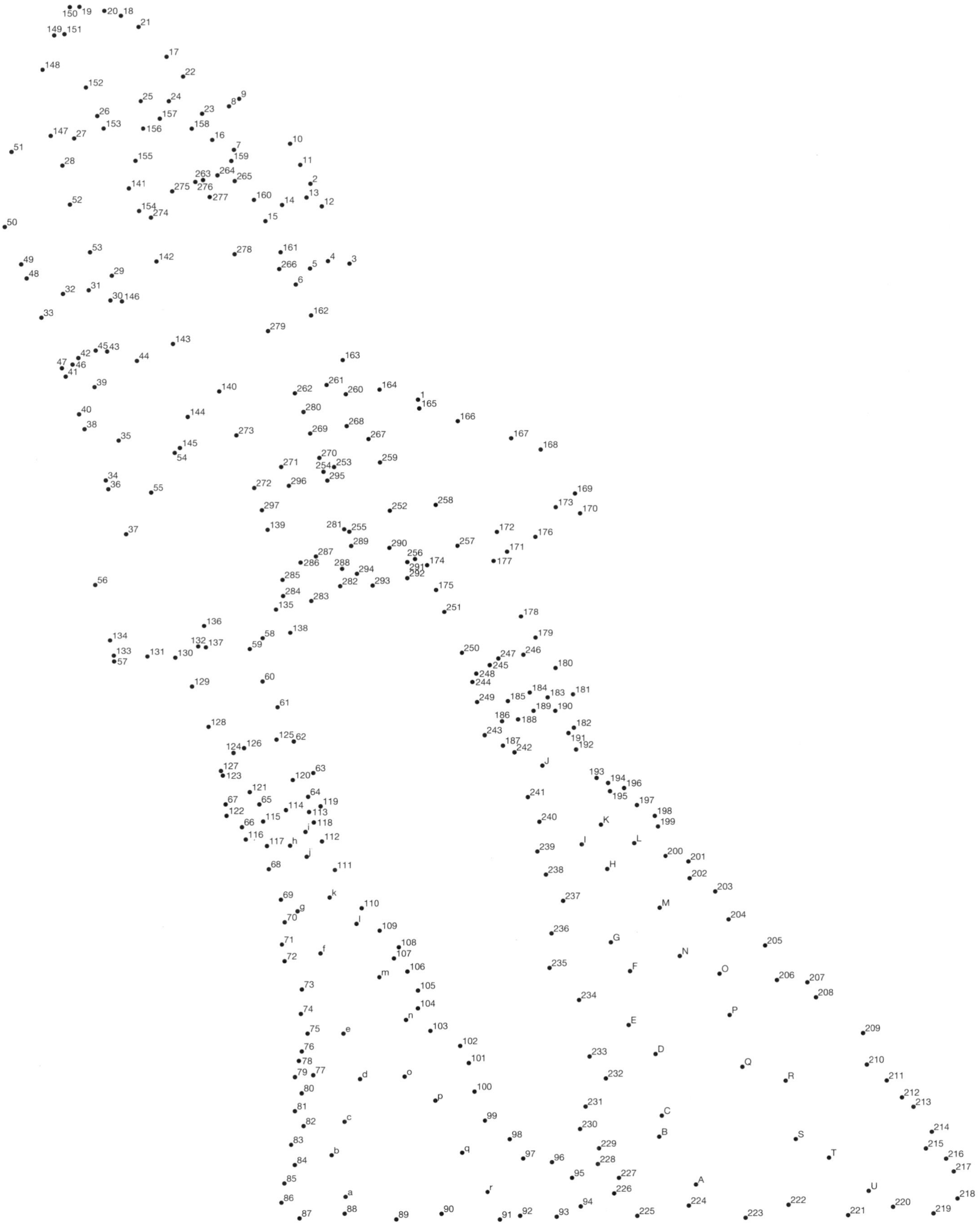

24

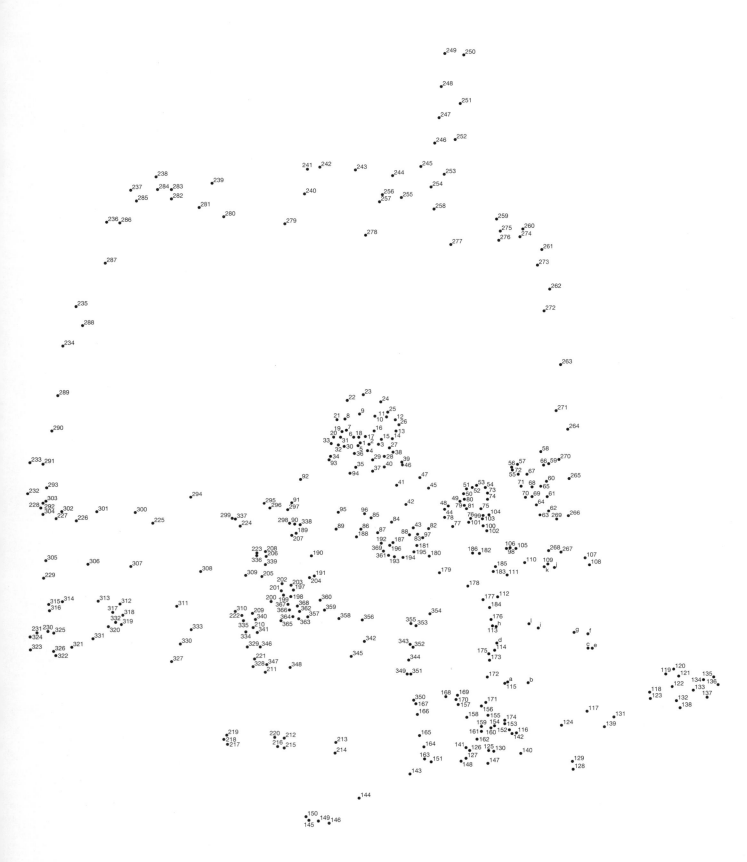

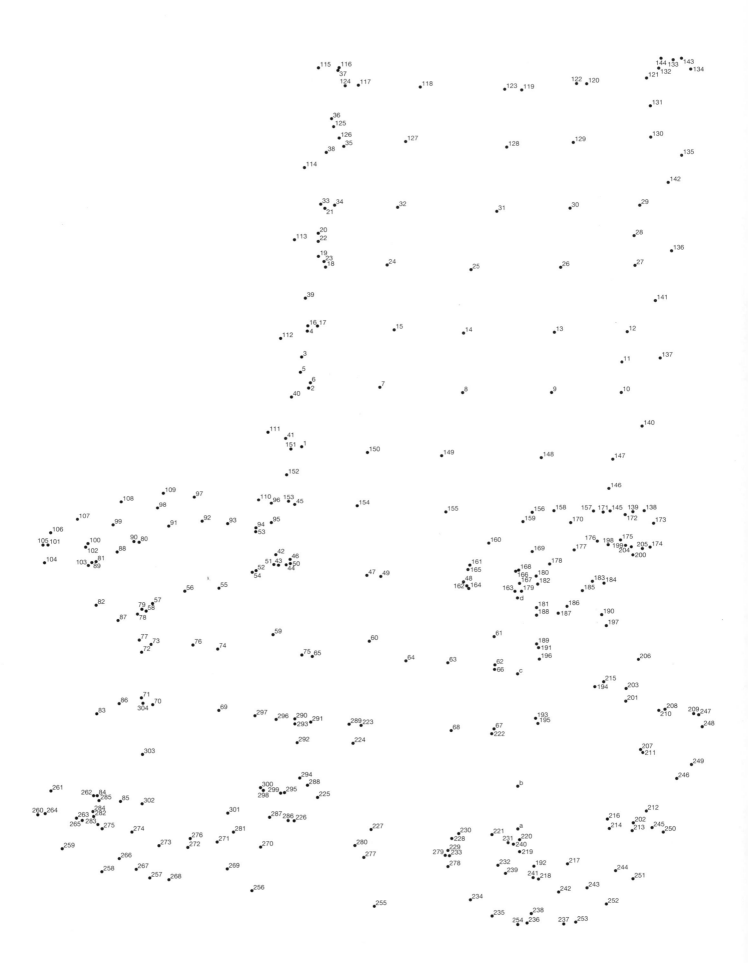

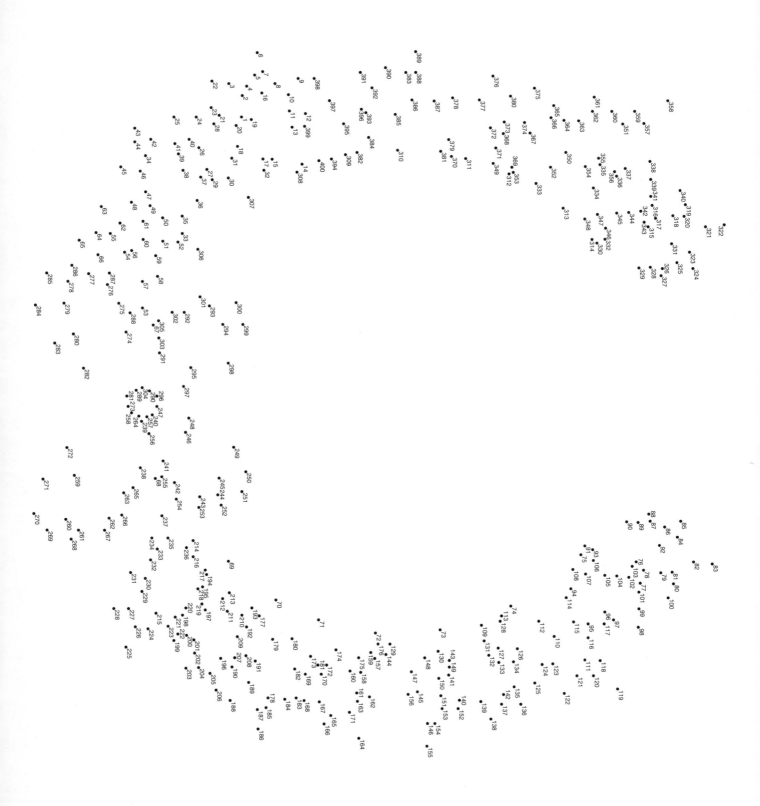

36

40

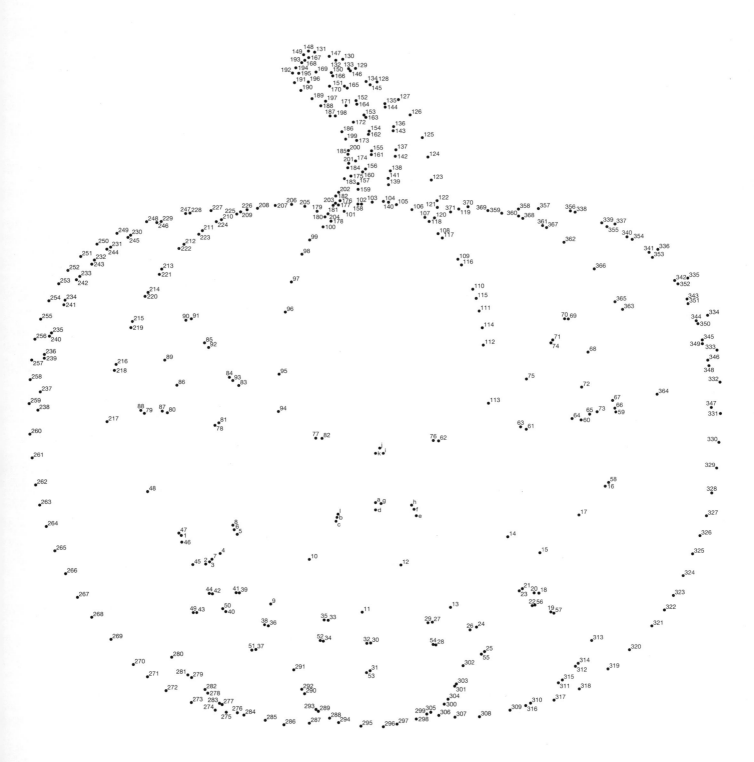

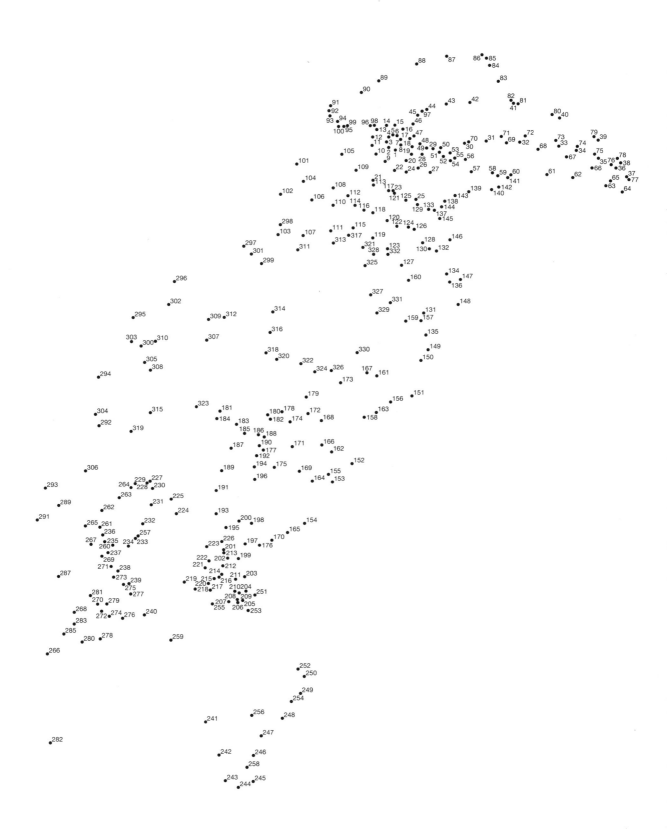

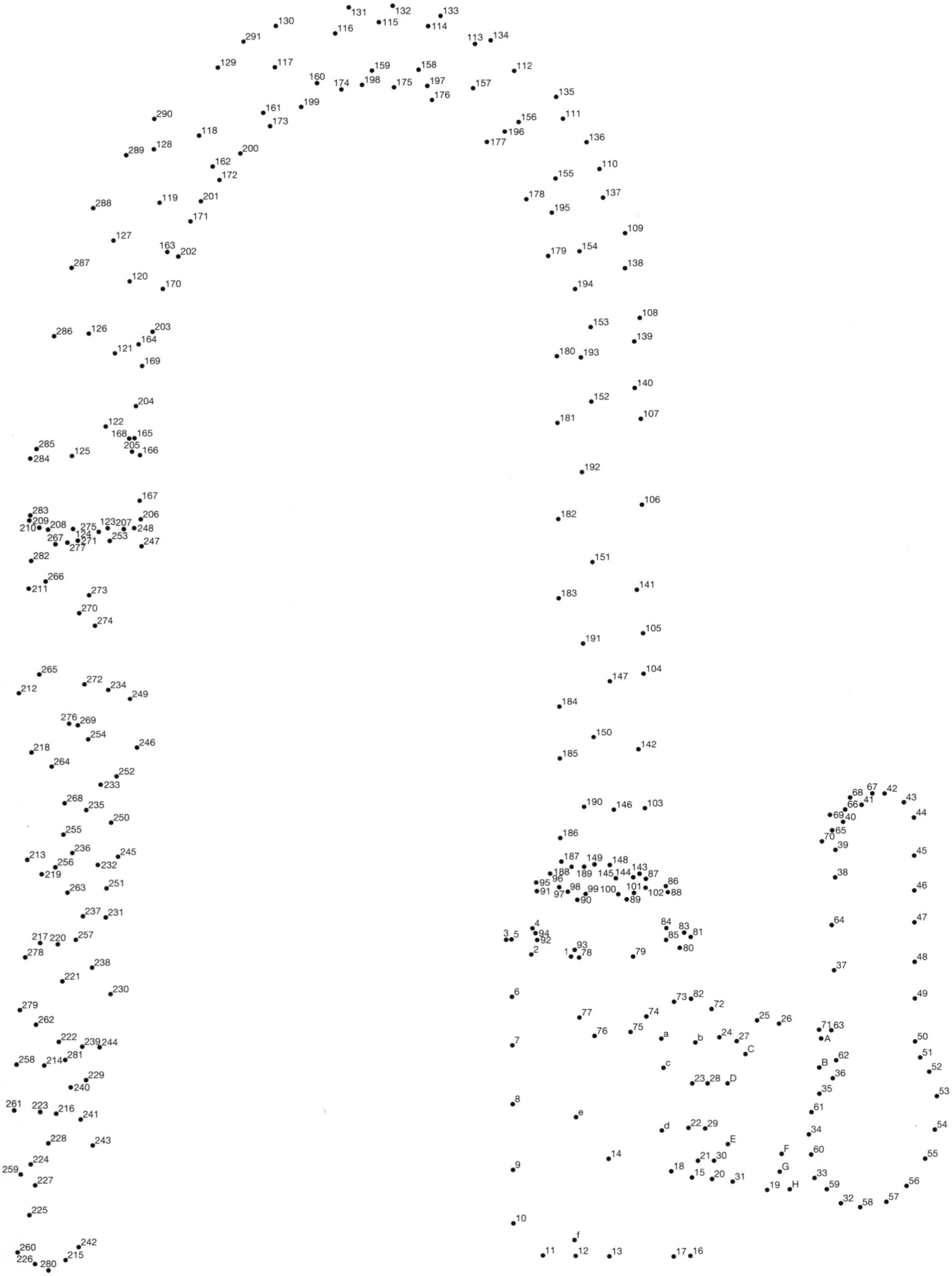

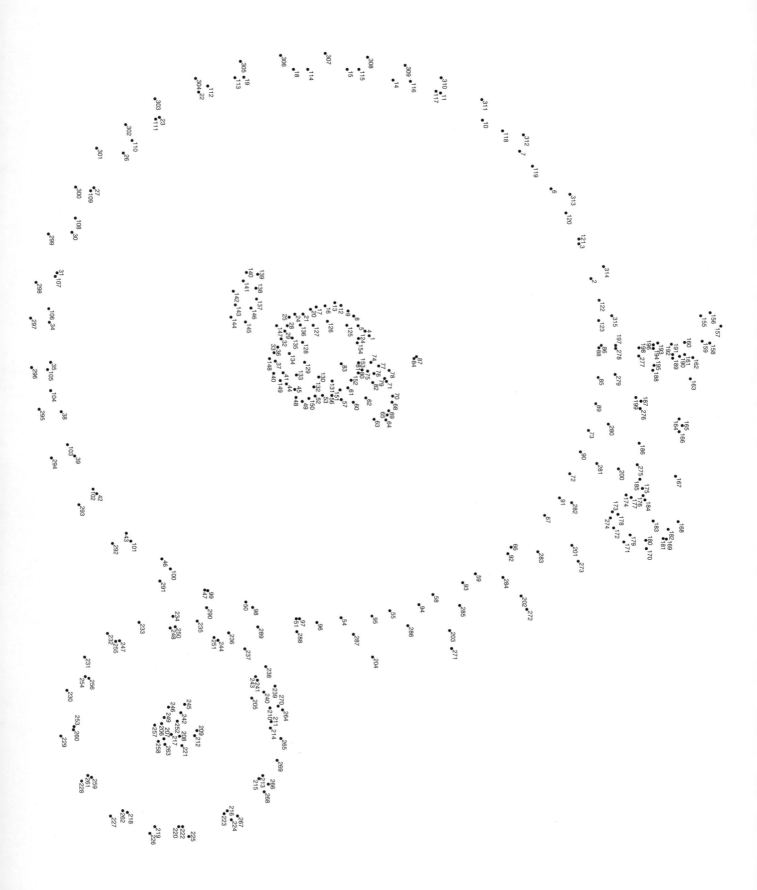

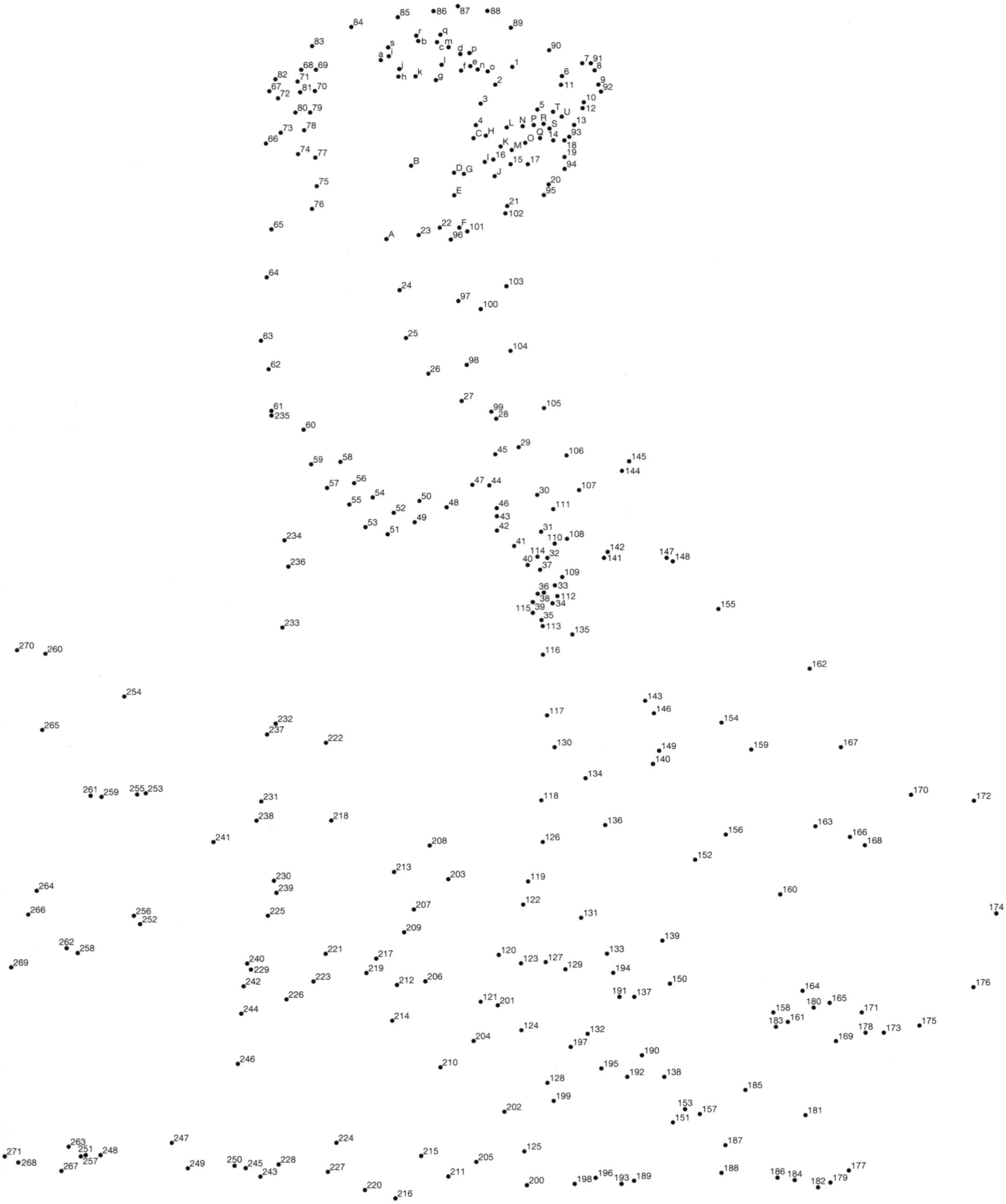

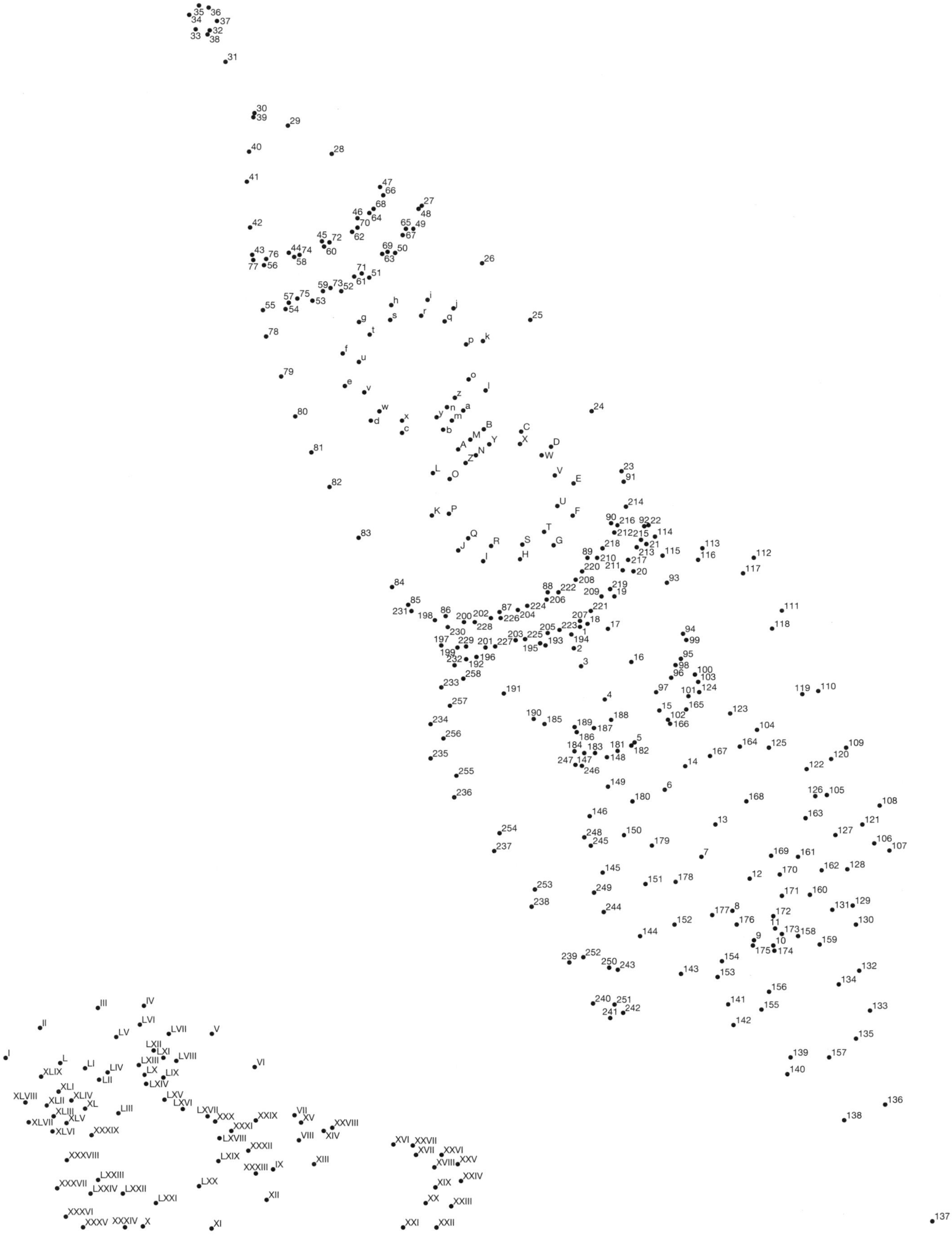

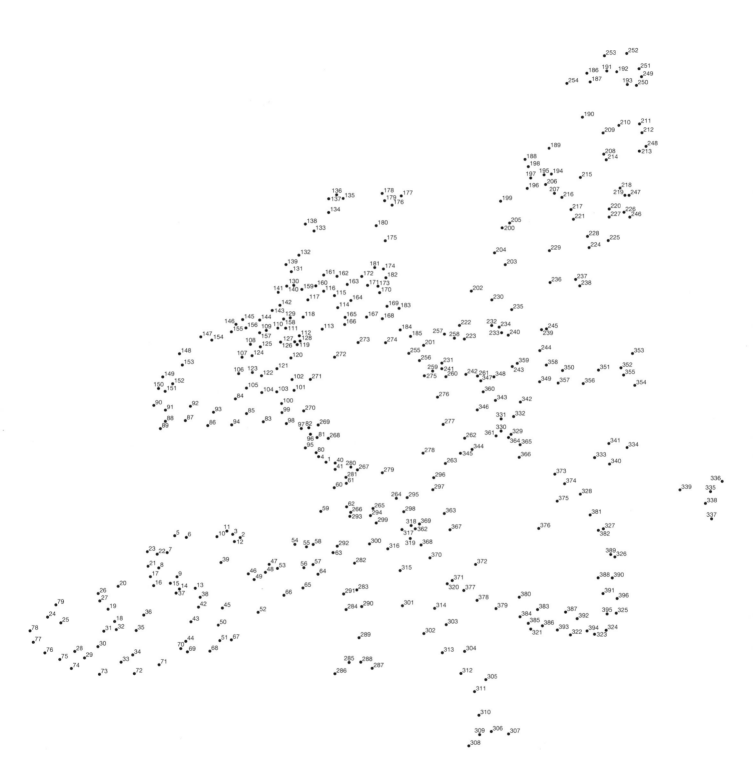

68

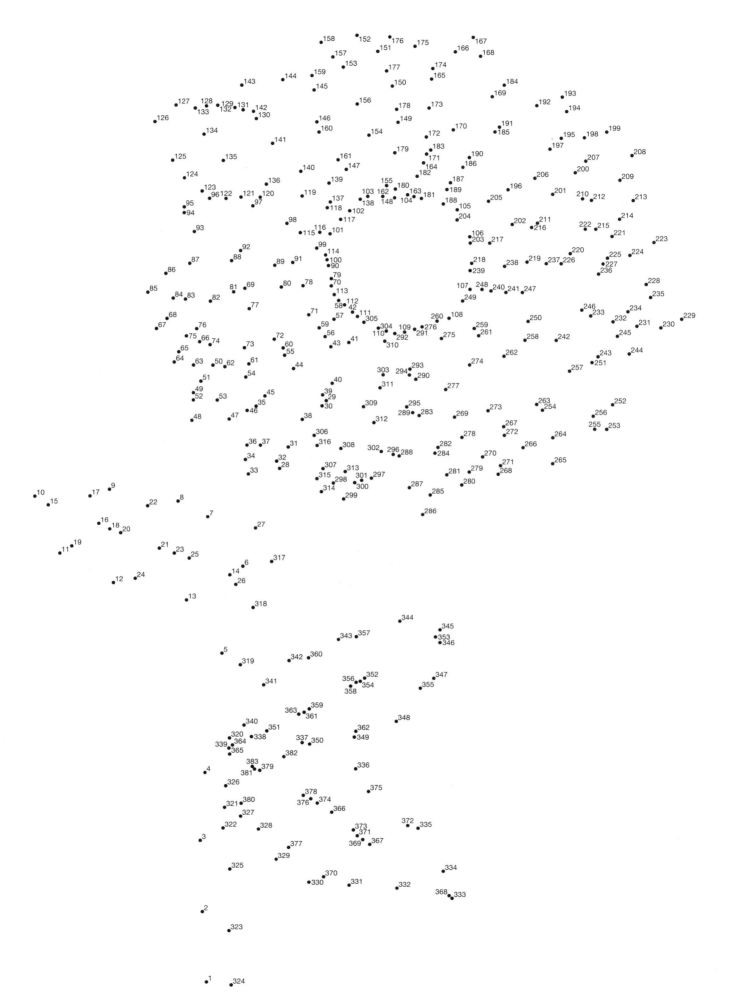

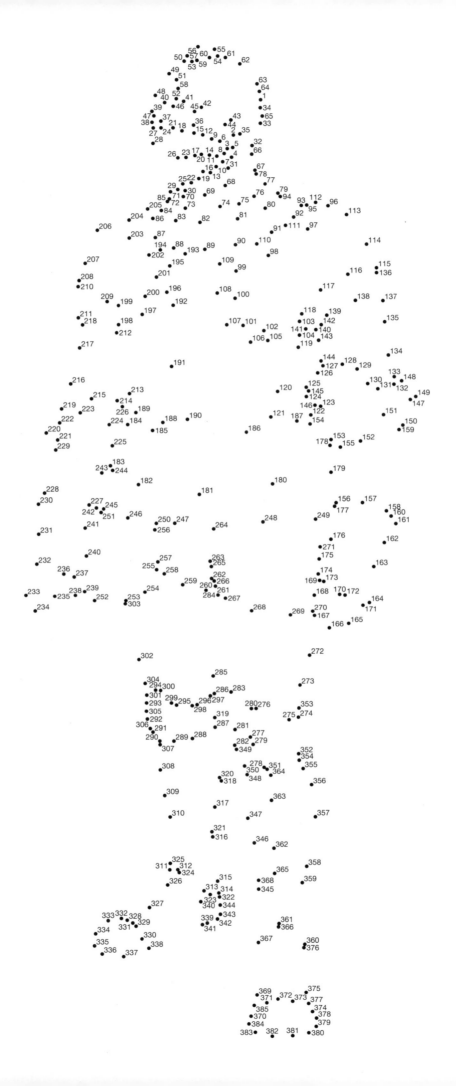

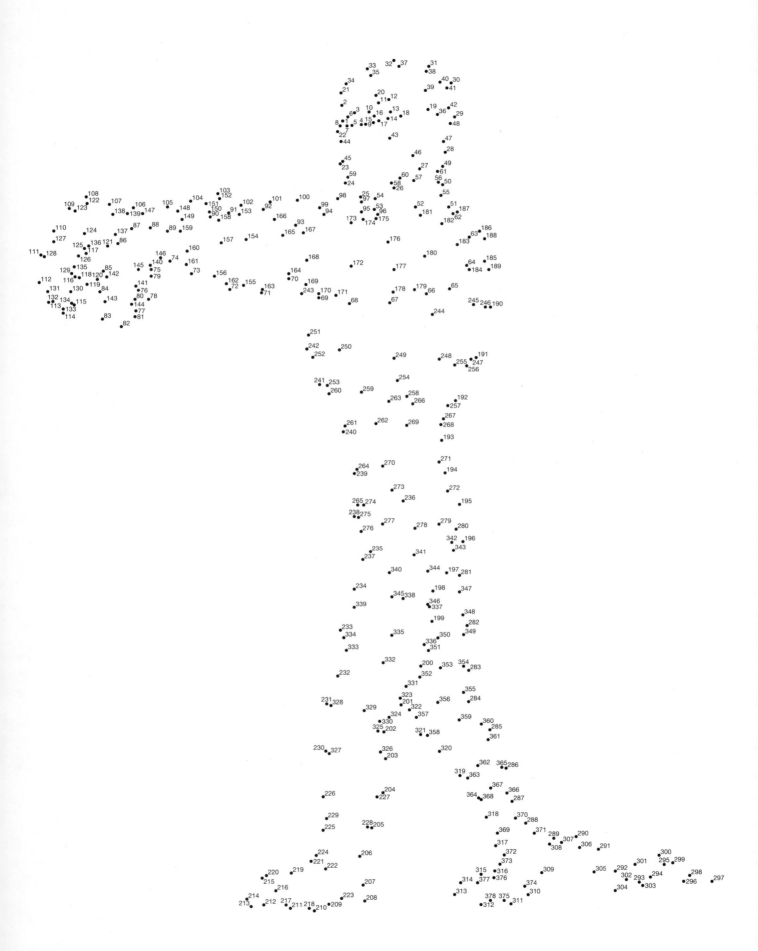

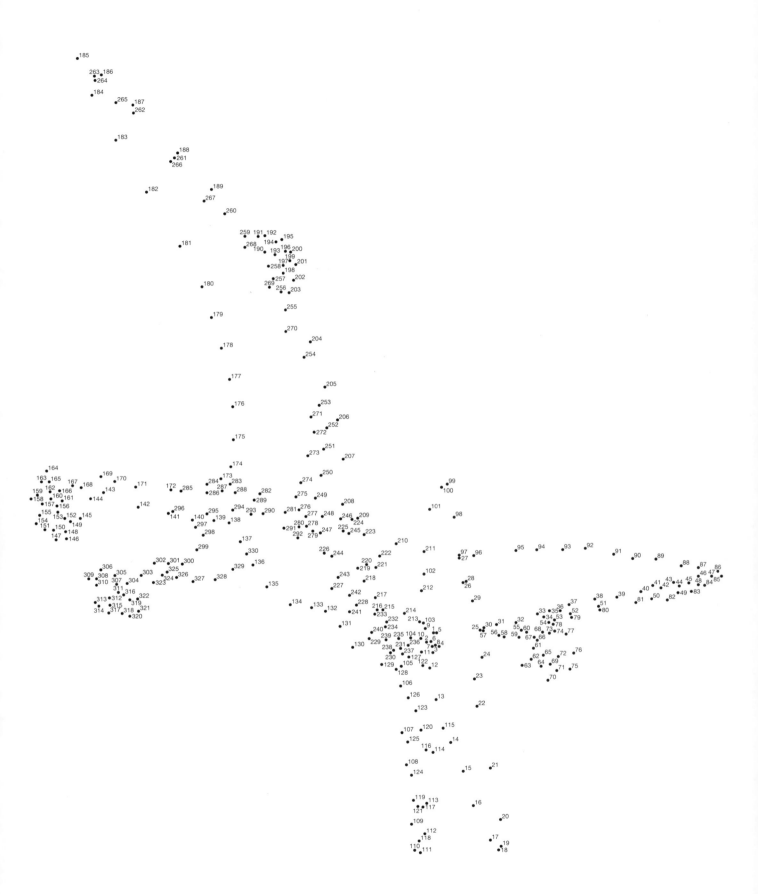

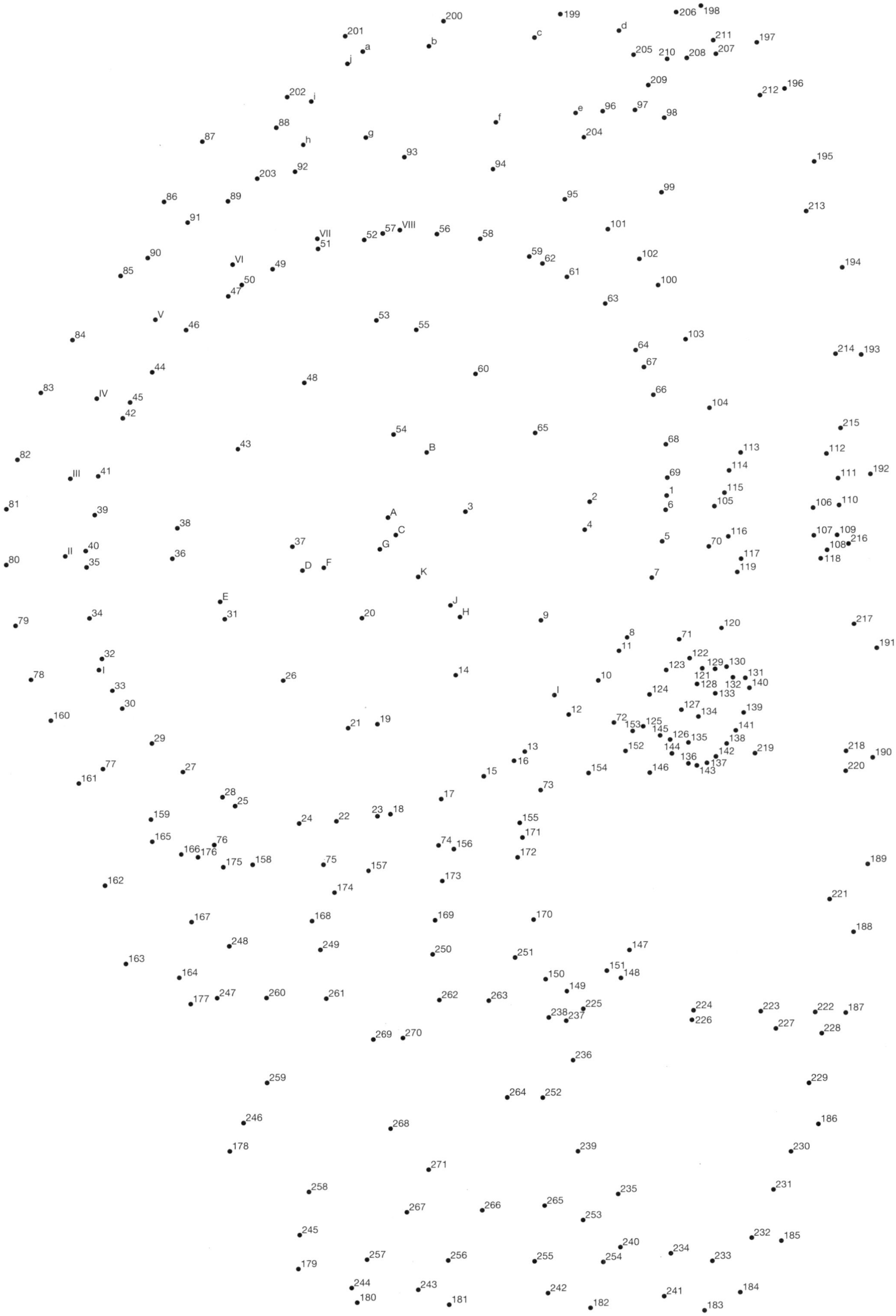

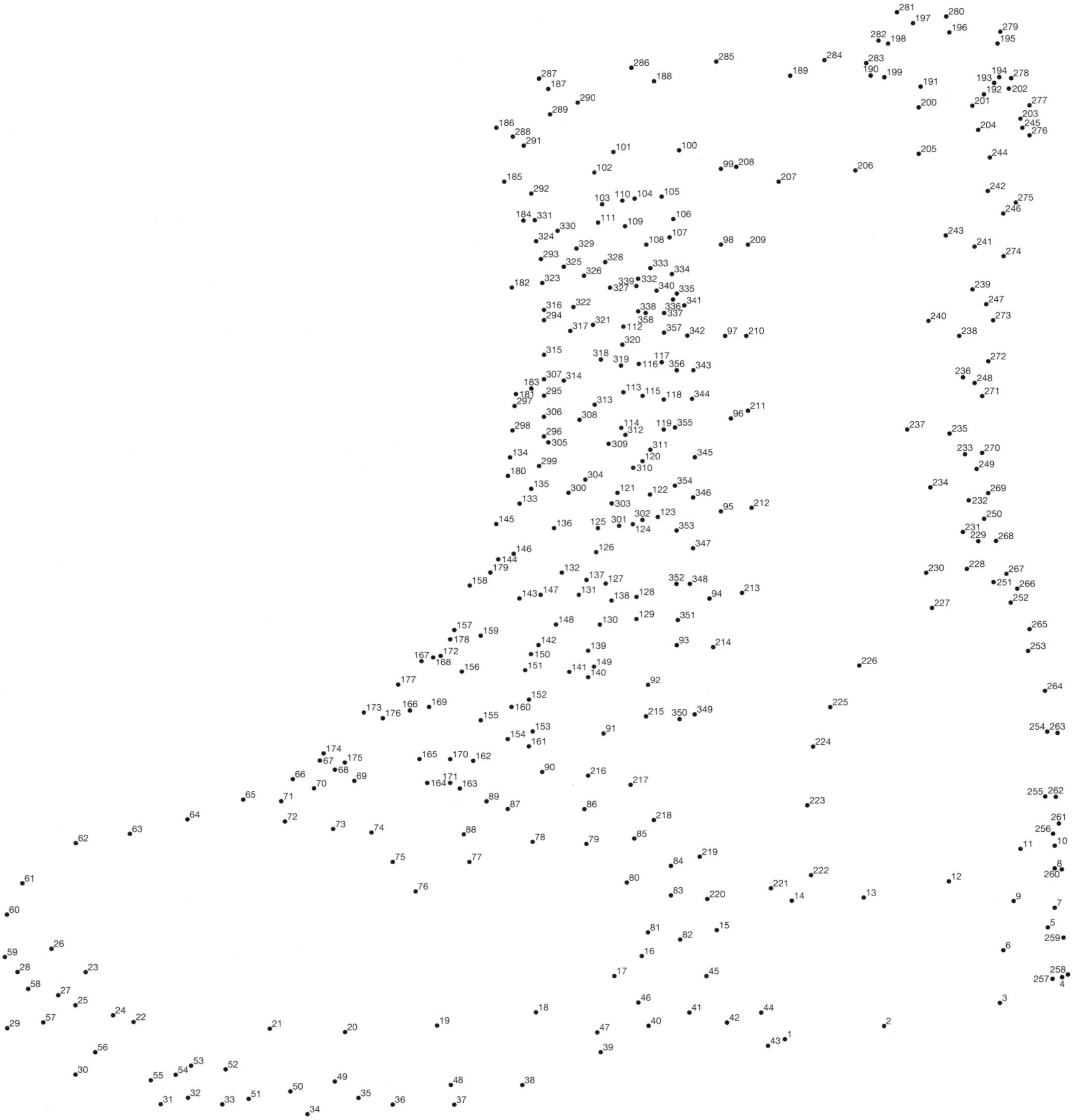

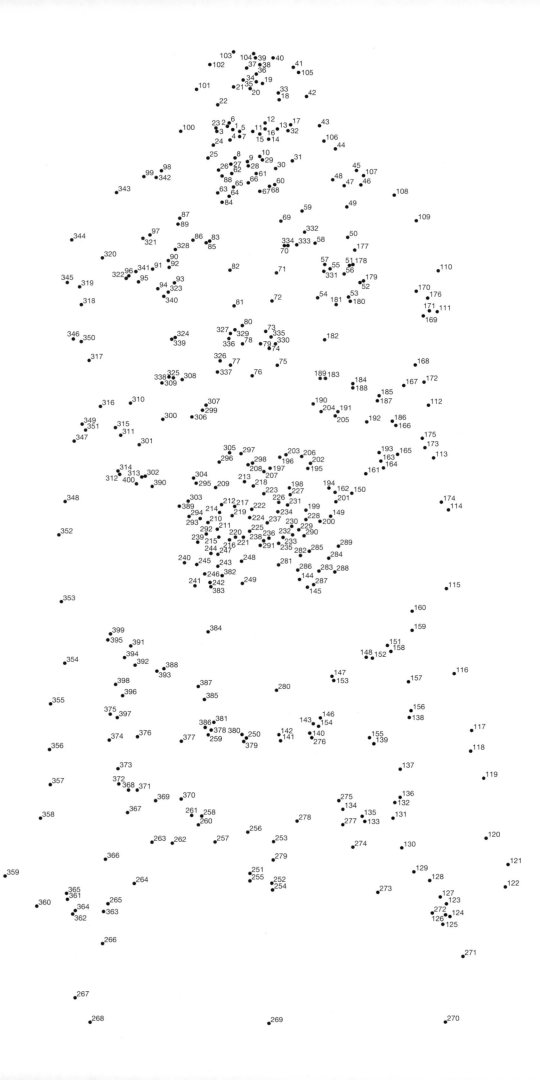

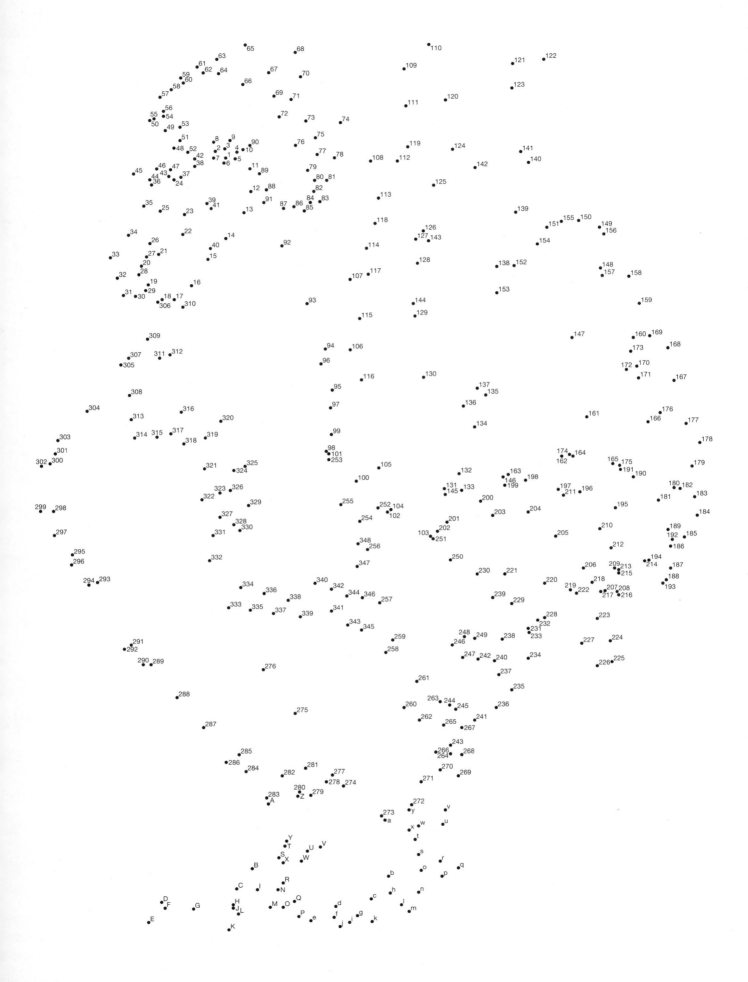

90

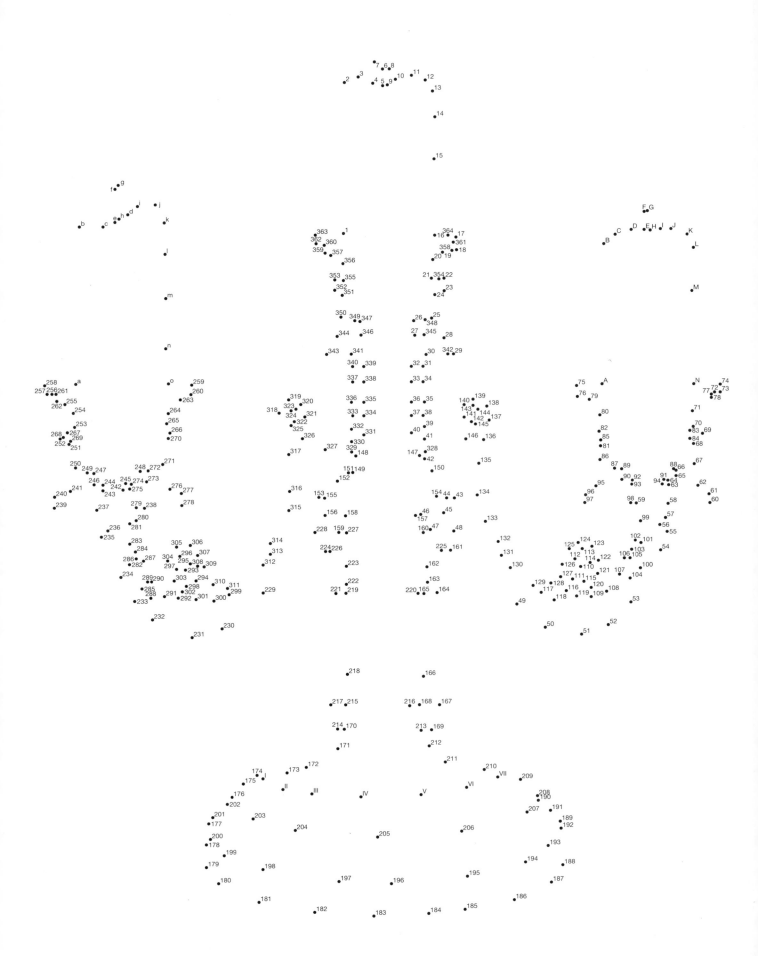

100

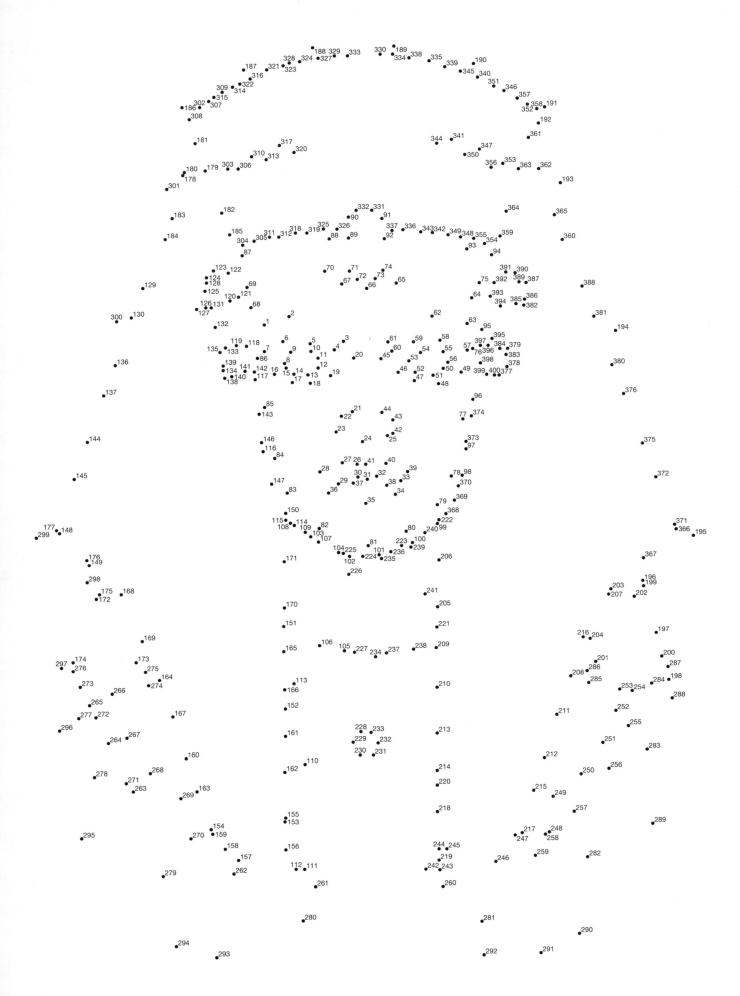

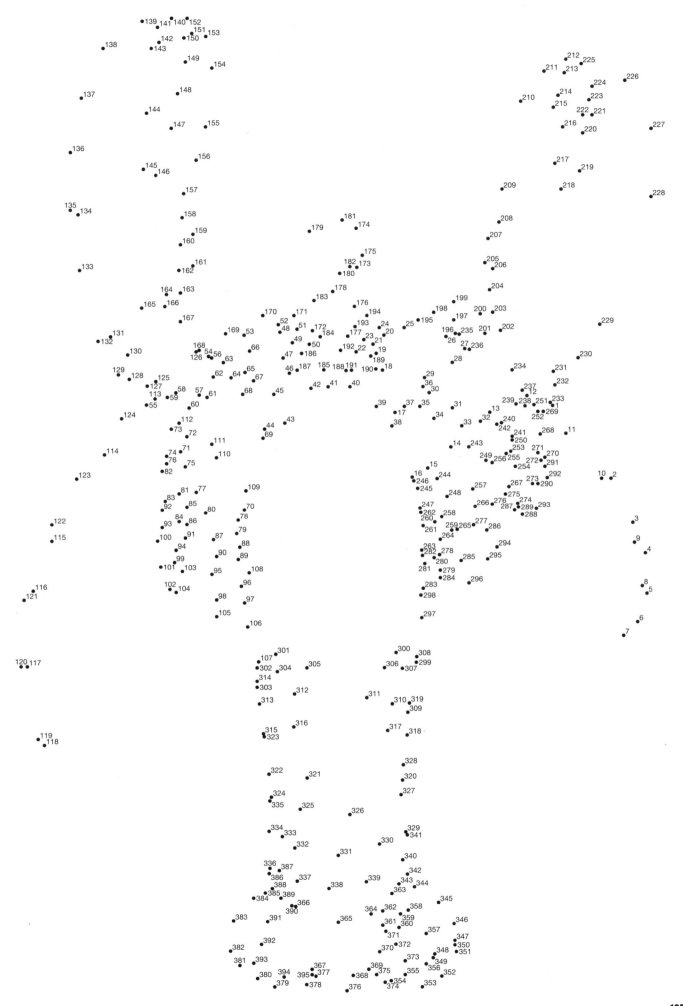

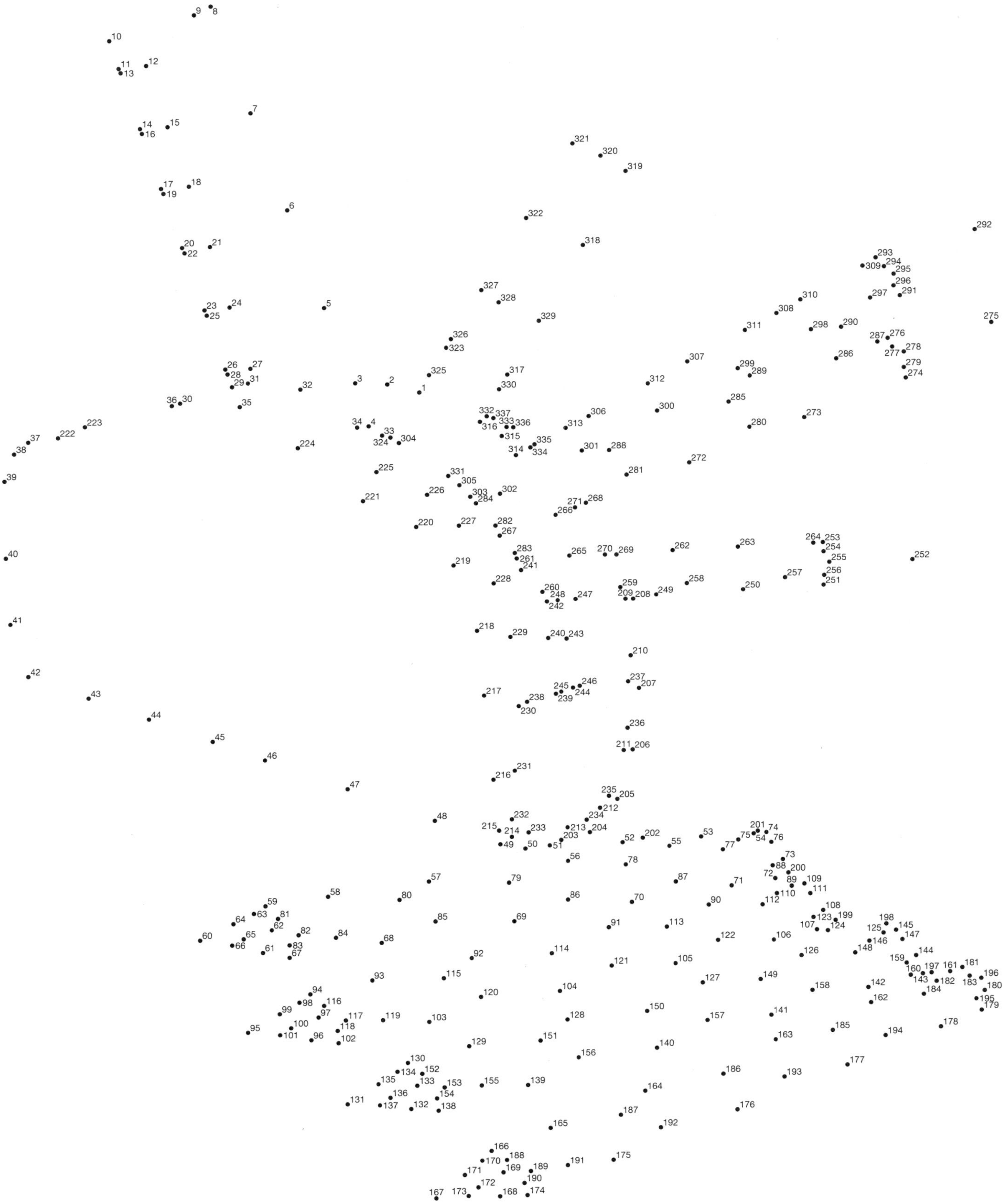

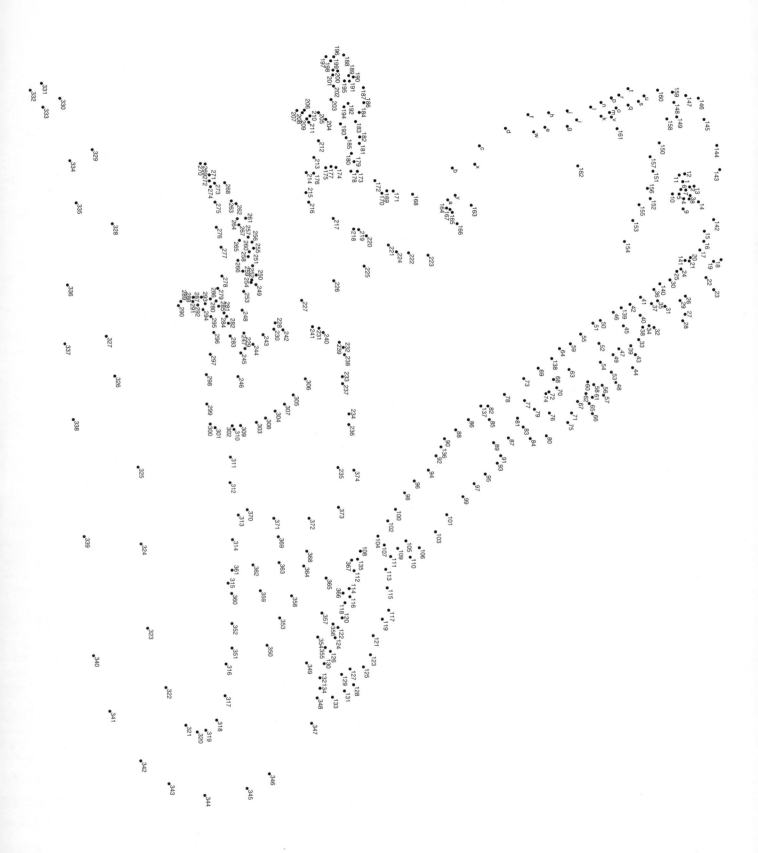

111

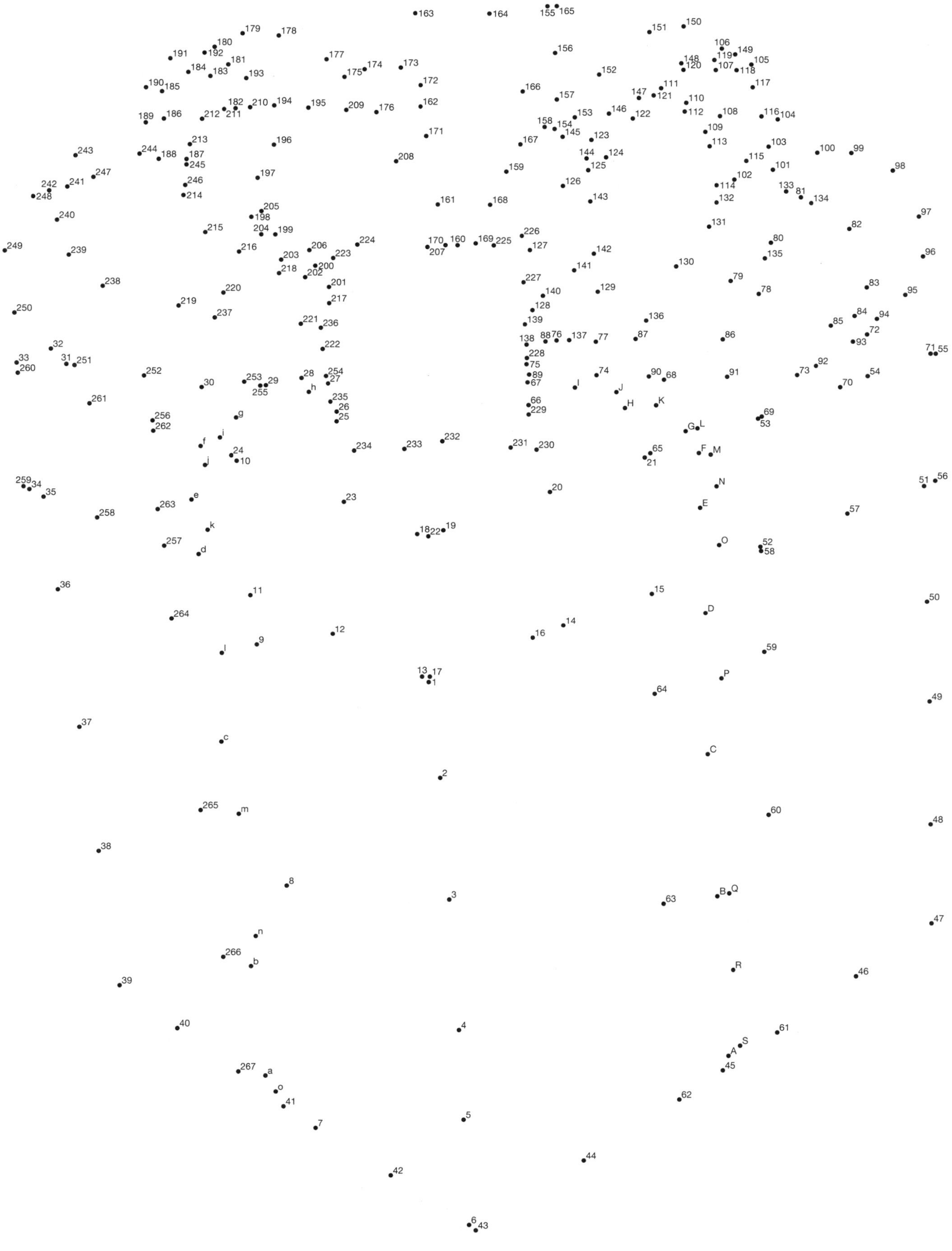

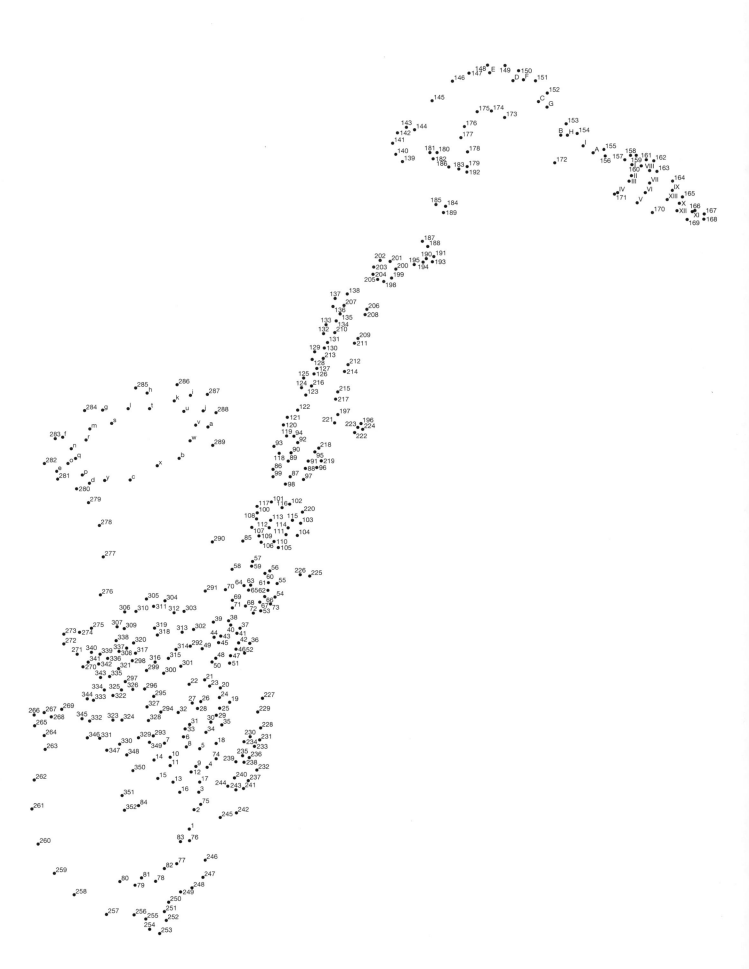

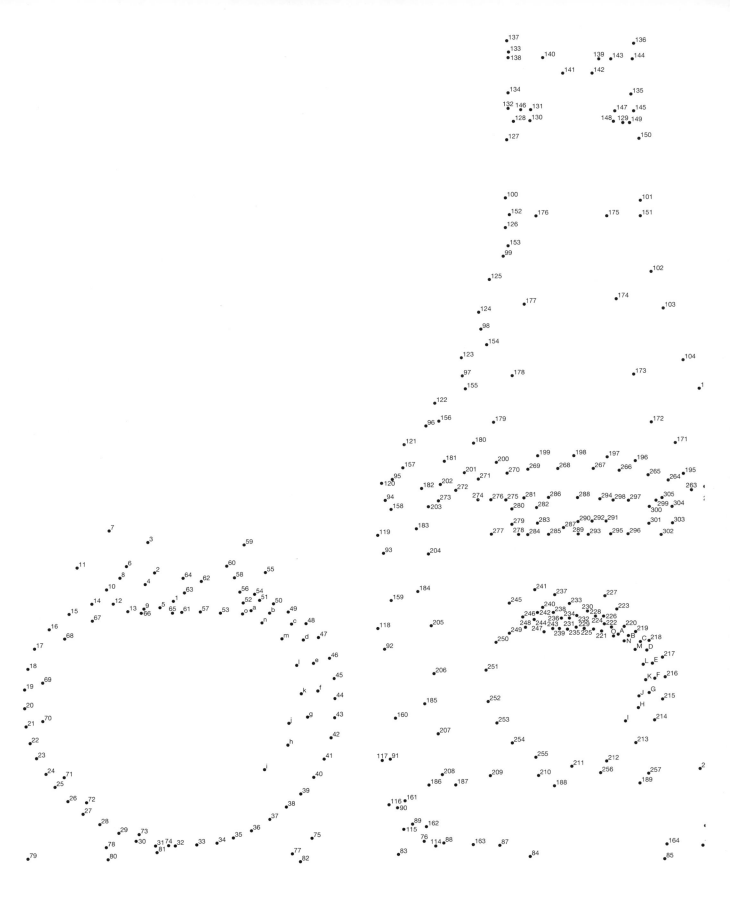

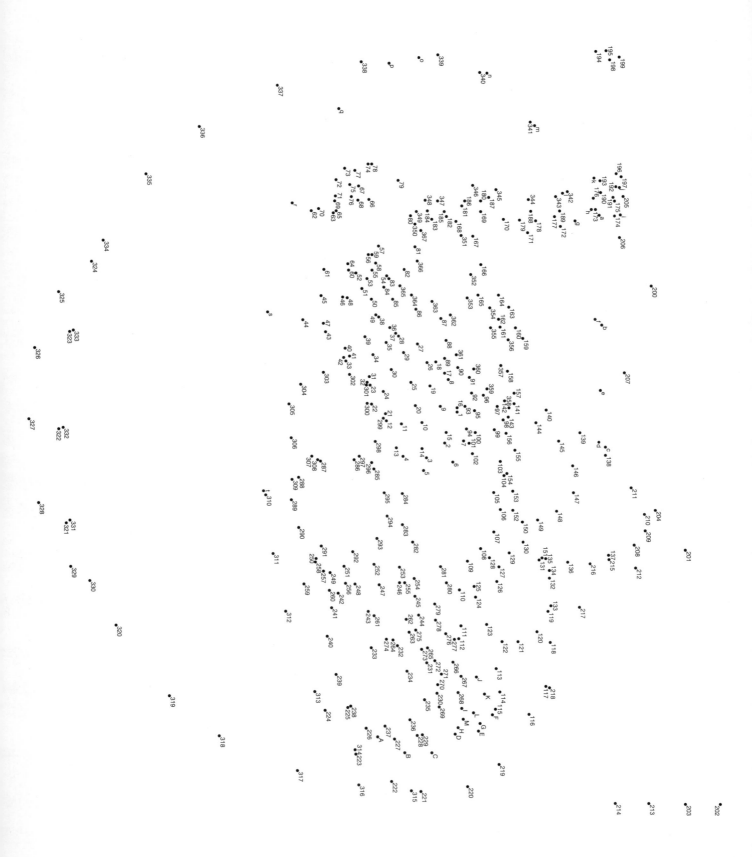

128

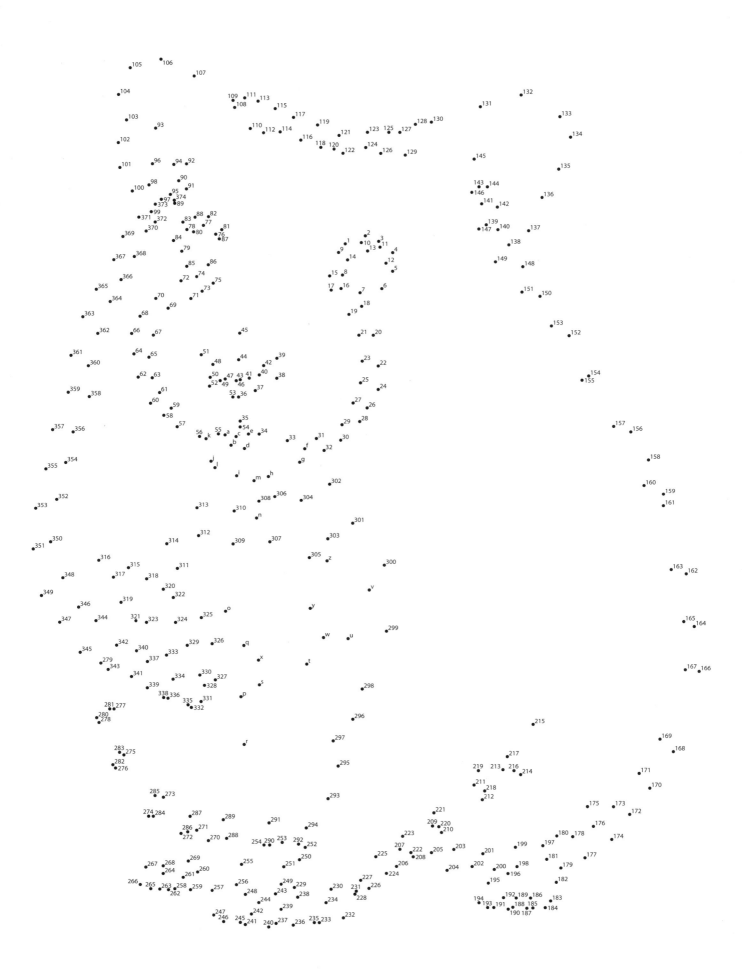

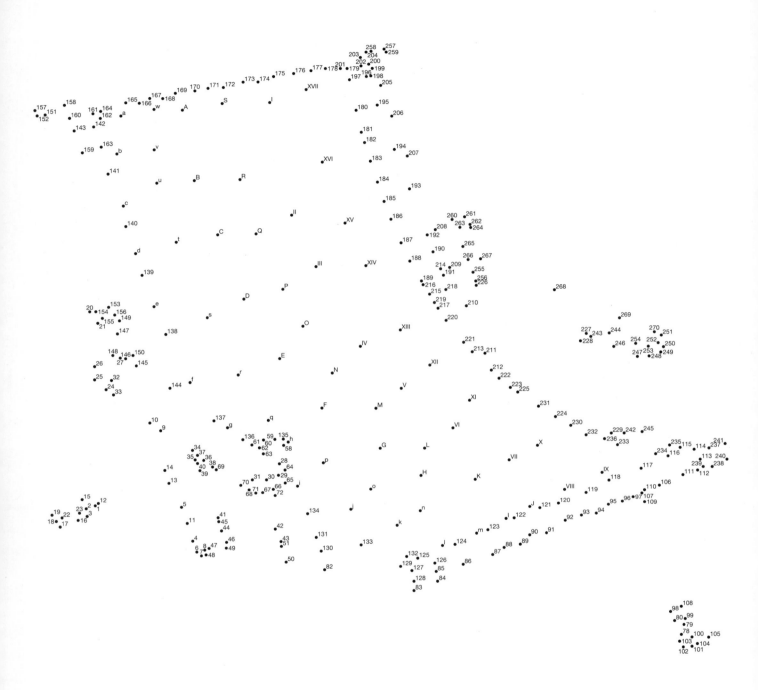

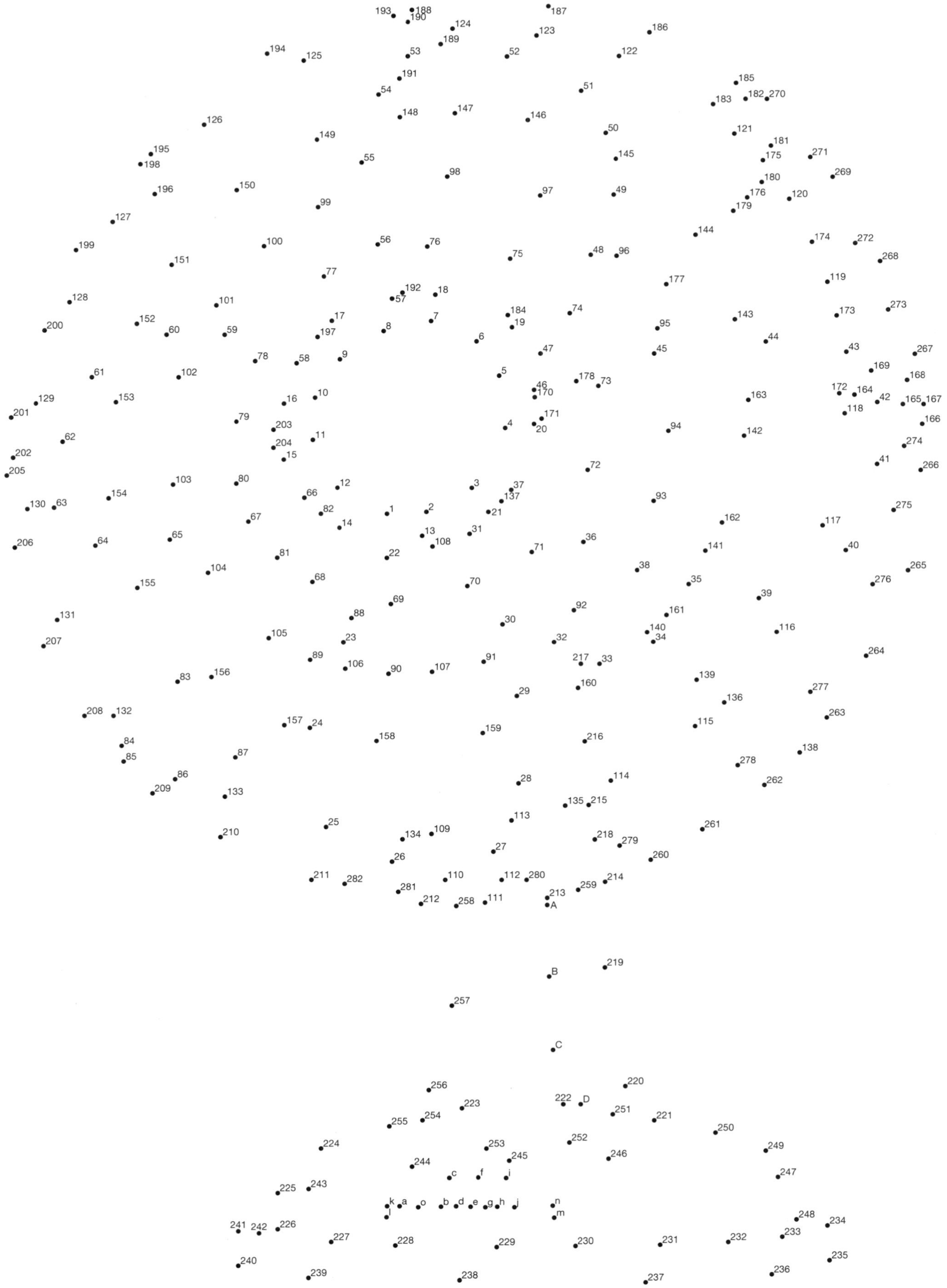

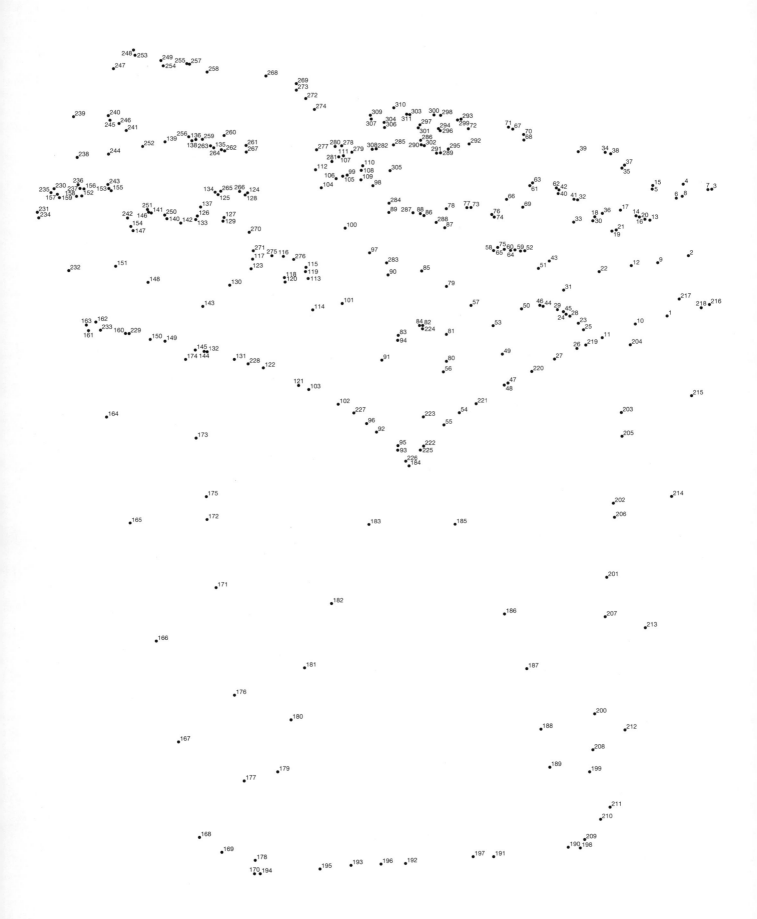

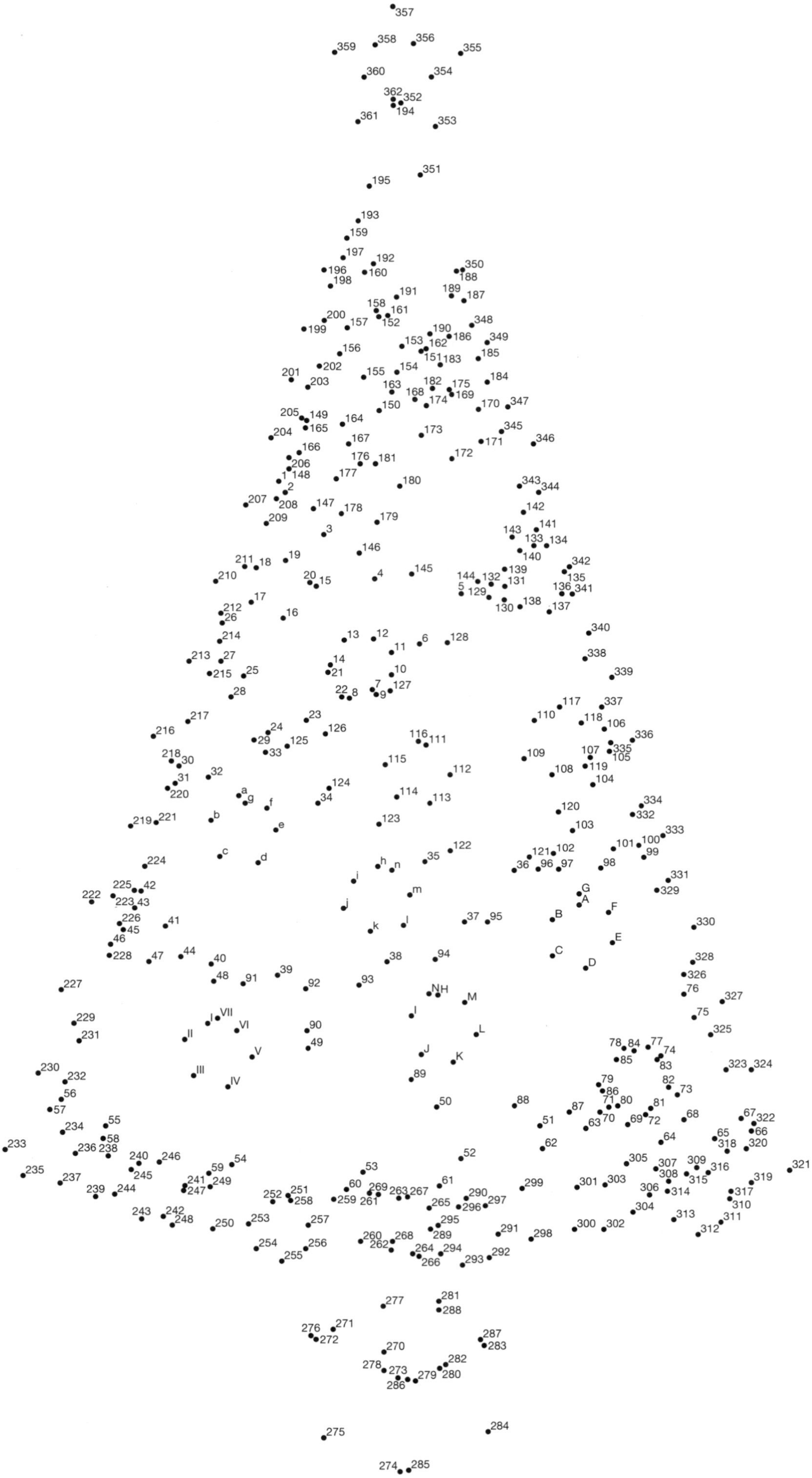

137

138

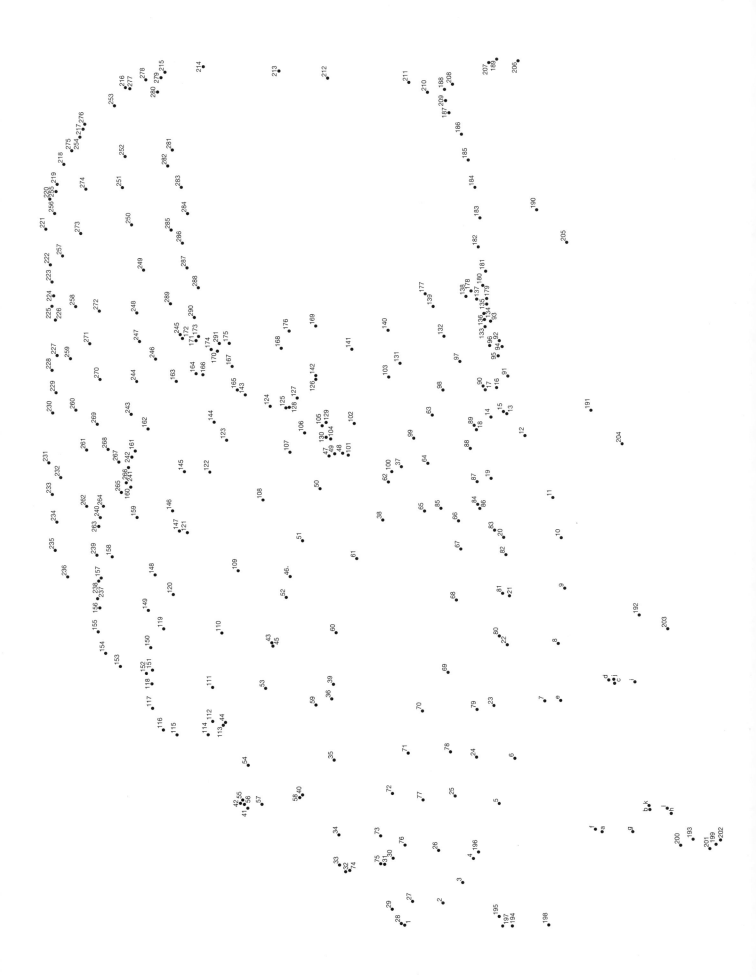

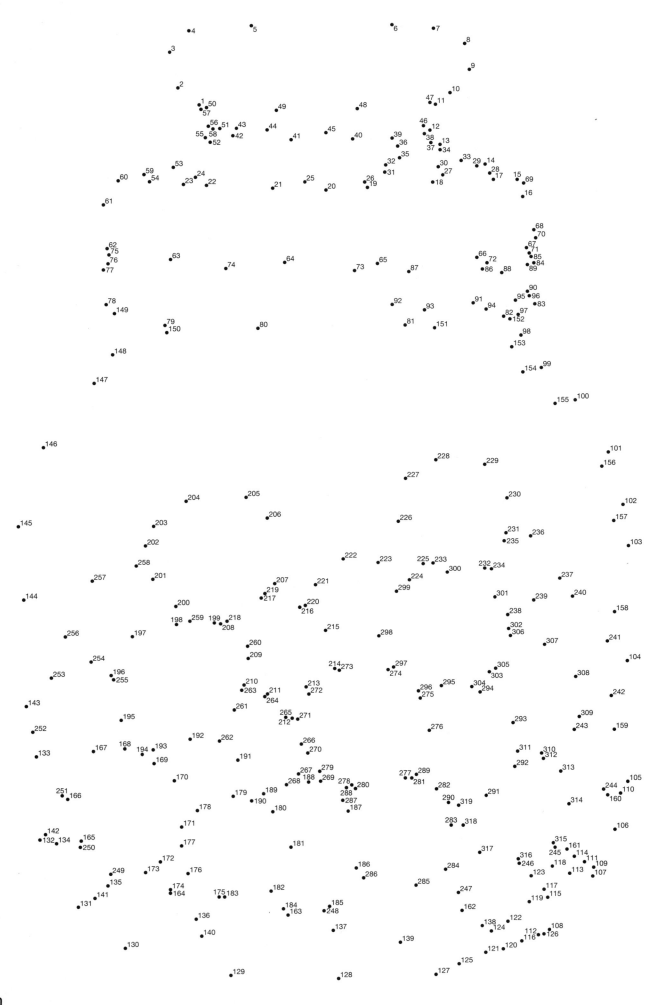

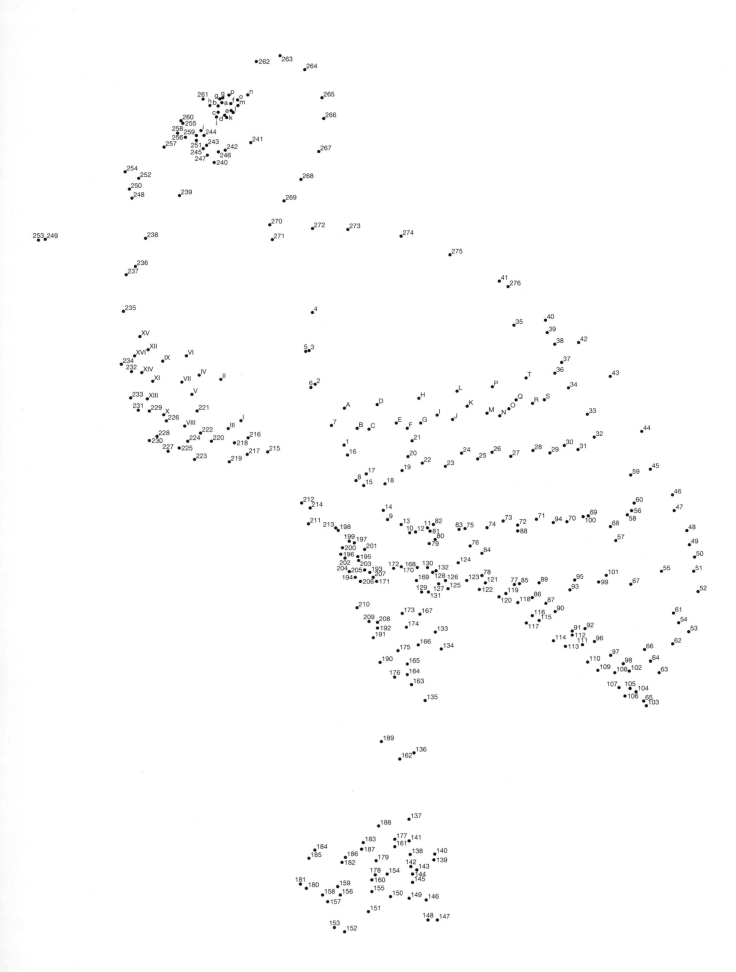

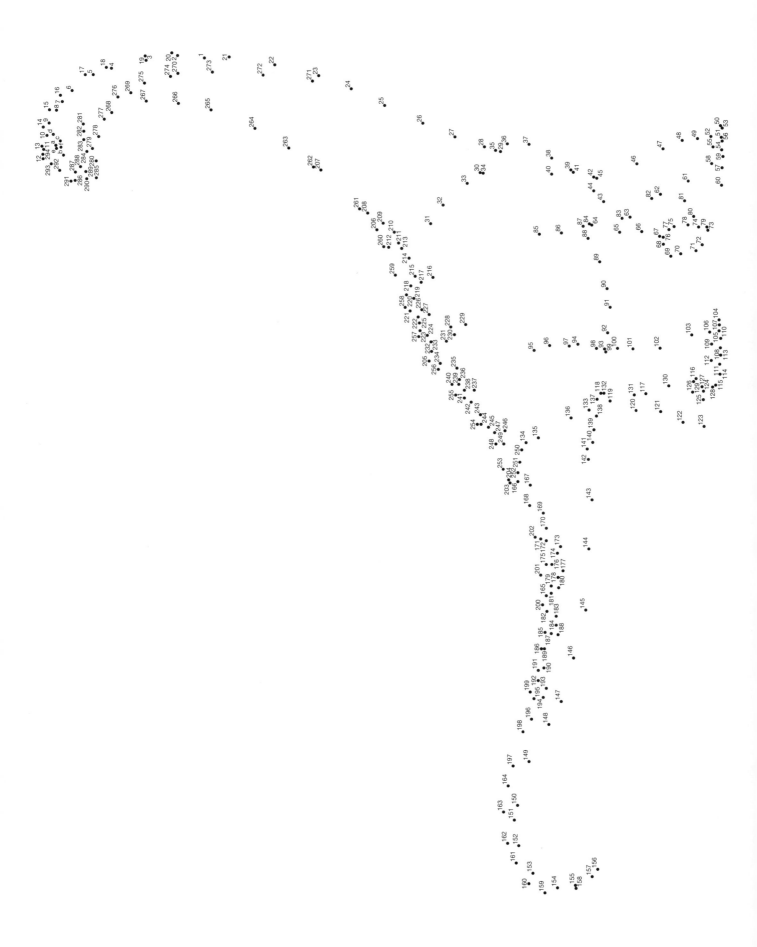

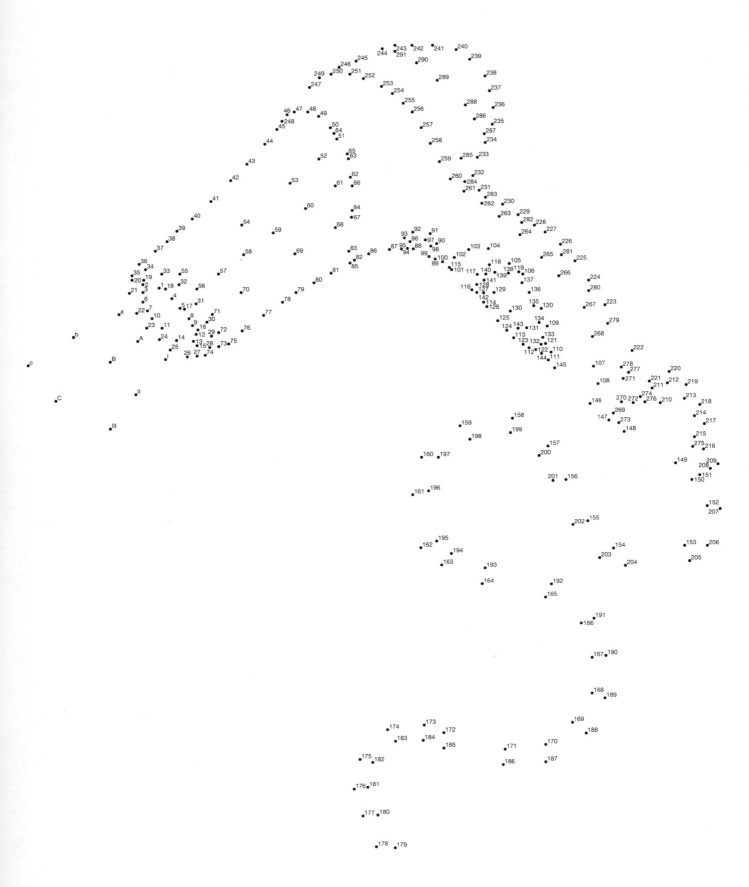

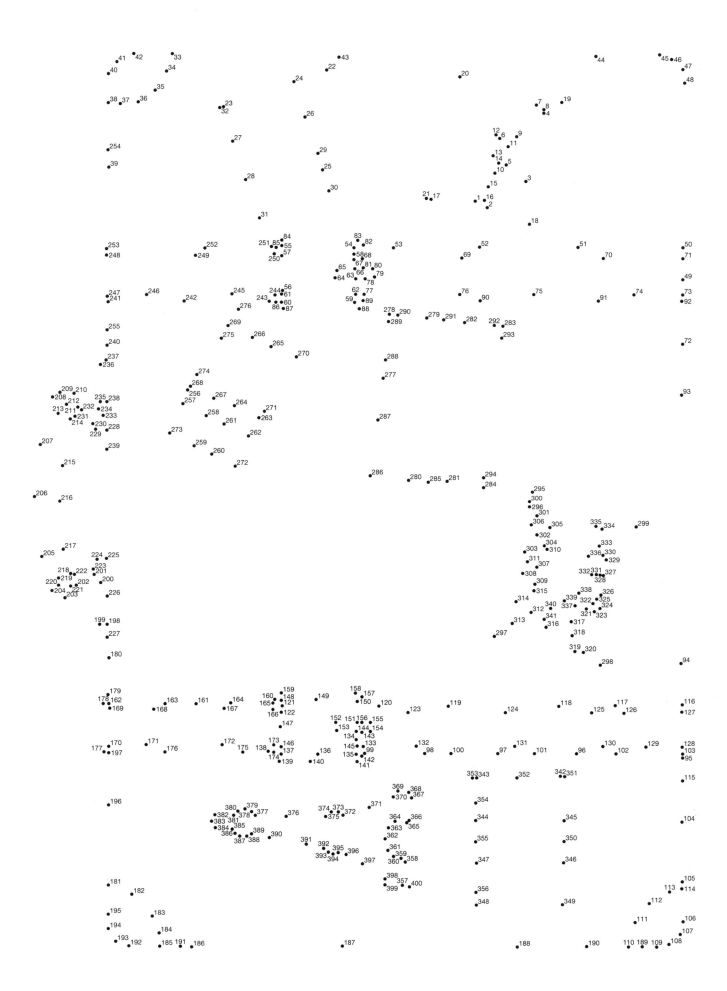

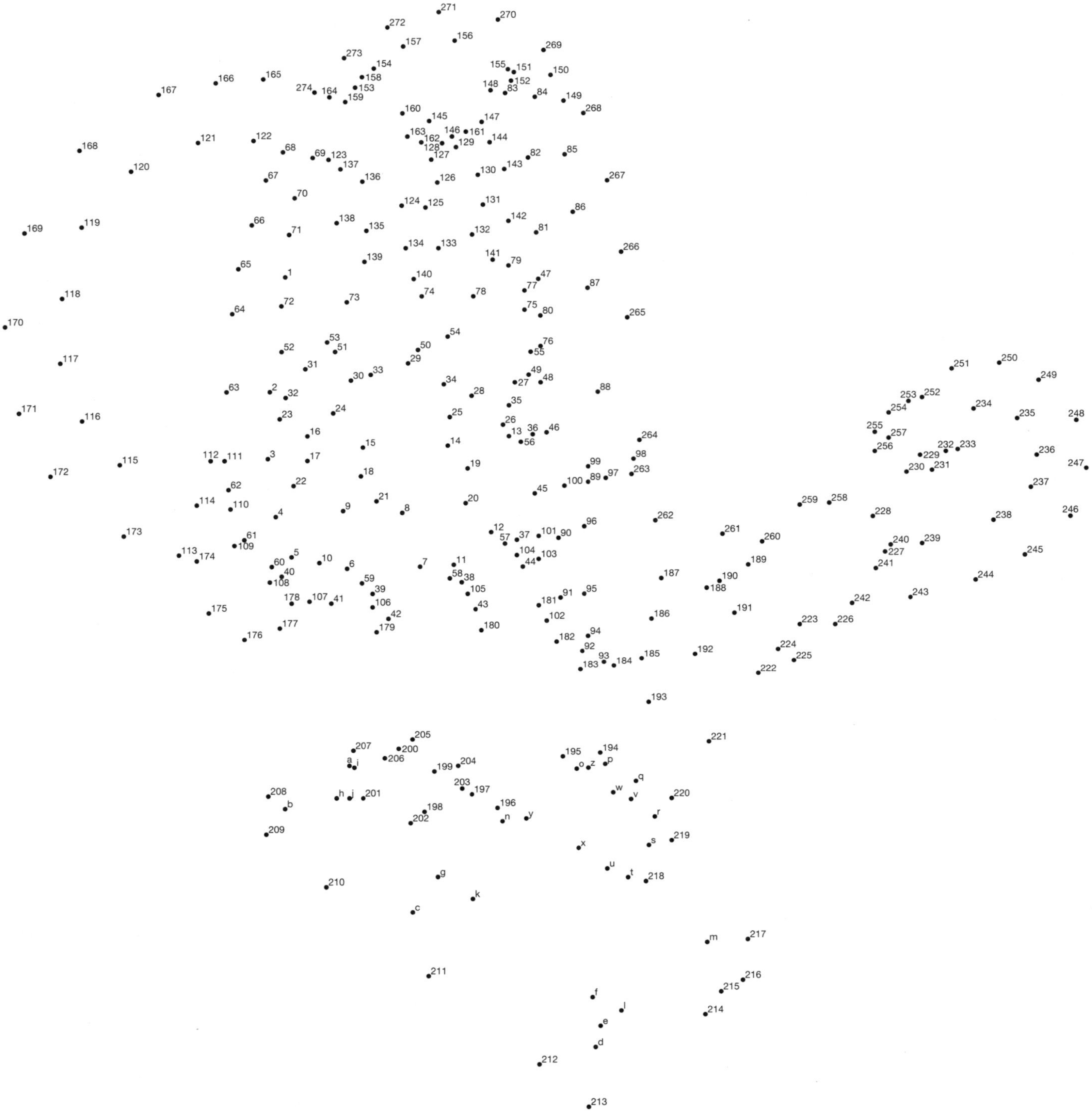

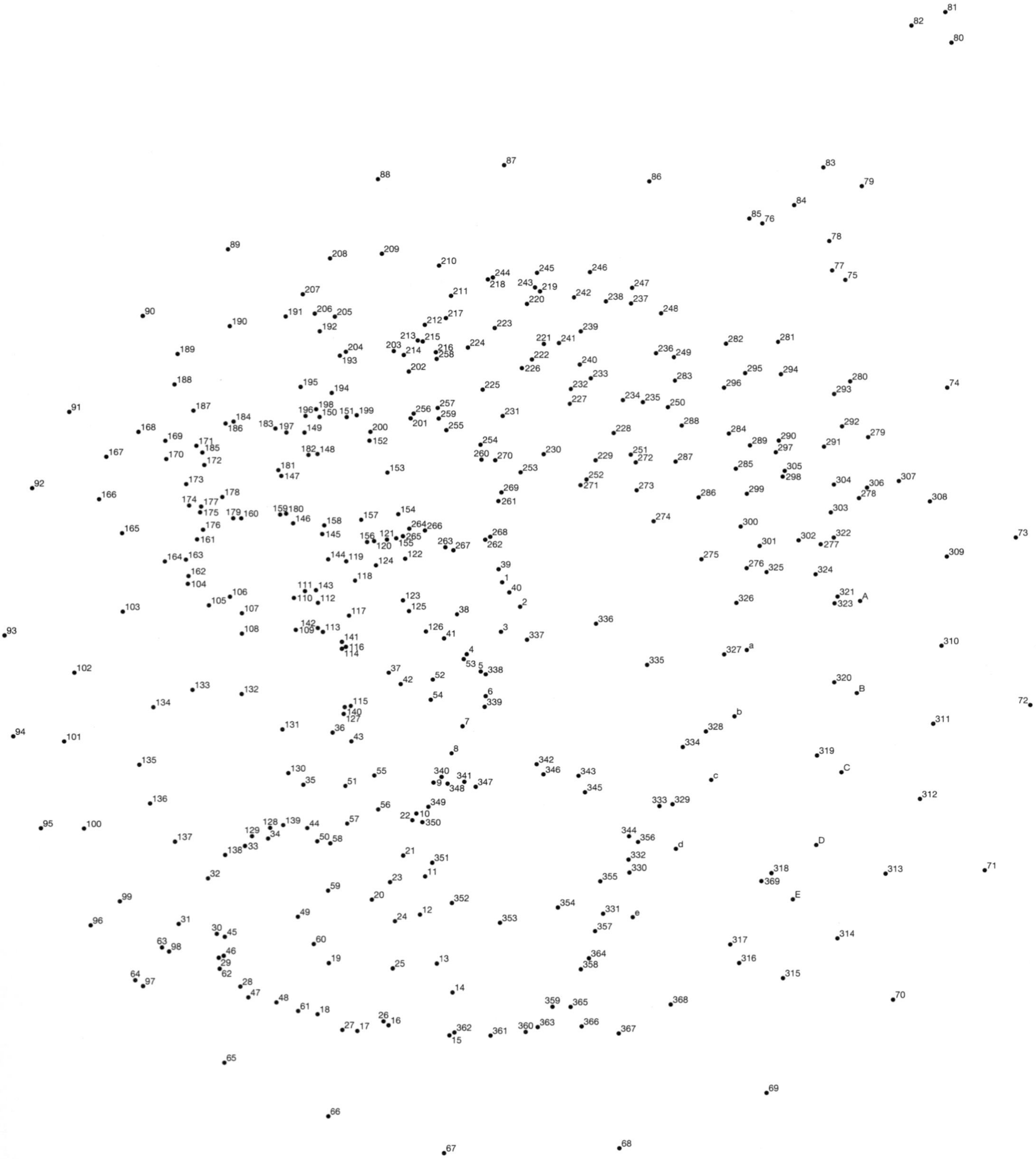

# LIST OF ILLUSTRATIONS